100 MEGA MACHINES
THE BIGGEST MACHINES EVER BUILT

100 MEGA MACHINES

THE BIGGEST MACHINES EVER BUILT

Richard Gunn

Bath · New York · Singapore · Hong Kong · Cologne · Delhi · Melbourne

First published in 2007
Parragon
Queen Street House
4 Queen Street
Bath BA1 1HE, UK

Copyright © Parragon Books Ltd 2007

ISBN 978-1-4054-8656-9

Editorial and design by
Amber Books Ltd
Bradley's Close
74–77 White Lion Street
London N1 9PF
www.amberbooks.co.uk

Project Editor: Sarah Uttridge
Design: Zoë Mellors and Hawes Design
Picture Research: Kate Green

Printed in China

Picture Credits

6(l): Getty (Hulton Archive), 6(tr): Philip Jarrett, 6(tmr): Getty (Time and Life Pictures), 6(bmr): Cody Images, 6(br): Bucyrus International Inc., 7(tl): Jensen Photo Collection, 7(tm): Photoshot/World Pictures, 7(tr): Cody Images, 7(b): Michael Williams, 8(l): Terex, 8(tr): Novosti, 8(br): Art-Tech/Aerospace, 9(t): Giles Chapman, 9(tl): Corbis (Lake County Museum), 9(ml): Robbins Company, 9(bl): Philip Jarrett, 9(r): Kempton Great Engine Trust (Peter Matthews), 10: Liebherr, 11(l): Amber Books (Mark Franklin), 11(r): Caterpillar, 12(both): Caterpillar, 13: Caterpillar, 14(both): Roadtec, 15: P&H Mining Equipment, 16: Trencor/Astec Underground, 17(both): Caterpillar, 18: Tower Cranes of America Inc., 19(both): Mammoet, 20: Andy Graves/andrewgraves.biz/ssc.htm, 21(t): Corbis (Reuters), 21(b): Richard Dredge, 22(t): Giles Chapman, 22(b): Getty Images (Jeff Haynes), 23(both): Koenig, 24: Richard Dredge, 25: April Martinez, 26(all): UPPA/Photoshot, 27(both): Gregory Dunham, 28: International Truck & Engine Corporation, 29(t), Getty Images, 29(b): International Truck & Engine Corporation, 30(both): Milepost 92½, 31: Brian Solomon, 32(both): Amtrak, 33(t): BAE Systems, 33(b): Cody Images, 34: Cody Images, 35: Cody Images, 36: Michael Williams, 37(both): John Deere/ASM Public Relations Ltd, 38(both): John Deere/ASM Public Relations Ltd, 39: Claas Lexion, 40(both): Caterpillar, 41: John Deere/ASM Public Relations Ltd, 42: Kalmar Industries AB, 43(both): Trans-Gesco, 44: Michael Williams, 45(both): Al Jon Inc., 46: AKG Images, 47 (both): Delta Queen Steam Boat Company, 48(t): Art-Tech/Aerospace, 48(b): Corbis (Hulton-Deutsch Collection), 49(t): Art-Tech/Aerospace, 49(b): Hagley Museum and Library, 50(t): Getty Images (Oleg Nikishin), 50(b): Getty Images (Laski Diffusion), 51: Cody Images, 52: Maersk Line, 53(t): US DOD/US Navy, 53(b): Corbis (Reuters), 54: Allseas Group, 55(both): US DOD/US Navy, 56(t): Corbis (Bettmann), 56(bl): Corbis (Bettmann), 56(br): Corbis (Dan Guravich), 57: Corbis (Dan Guravich), 58: Thomas McConville (AP), 59: Getty Images (Frank Perry), 60: Getty Images (Mario Tama), 61: Royal Caribbean, 62(t): Rex Features (News (UK) Ltd), 62(b): Rex Features (Sipa Press), 63(t): MARS, 63(b): Philip Jarrett, 64(both): Getty Images, 65(t): Getty Images (Peter McBride), 65(b): Philip Jarrett, 66: Philip Jarrett, 67(both): Philip Jarrett, 68(t): Philip Jarrett, 68(b): US DOD/USAF, 69(both): Art-Tech/Aerospace, 70: Art-Tech/Aerospace, 71(b): Cody Images, 71(b): Airbus, 72(both): NASA/Dryden Flight Research Center, 73: US DOD/USAF, 74: US DOD/USAF, 75(t): Philip Jarrett, 75(b): Art-Tech/Aerospace, 76(t): Corbis (Peter Turnley), 76(b): Corbis (Stringer/epa), 77(both): US DOD, 78(l) Corbis, 78(r): Amber Books, 79: Corbis (Roger Ressmeyer), 80: NASA, 81(t): Art-Tech/Aerospace, 81(b): NASA, 82: Art-Tech/Aerospace, 83(t): NASA, 83(b): Chandra/Harvard, 84: Art-Tech/Aerospace, 85(both): ESA, 86(both): NASA, 87: NASA, 88(t): Corbis (Jim Sugar), 88(b): Corbis (Gene Blevins), 89(both): NASA/JPL-CalTech, 90: General Electric Company, 91: Wärtsila Switzerland Ltd, 92: Sony, 93(both): Duluth Seaway Port Authority, 94: Corbis (Alex Steedman), 95(t): Corbis (Ben Wood), 95(b): Corbis (Dave Bartruff).

CONTENTS

CLOCKWISE: The V2 rocket developed in 1932, saw the start of modern rocket warfare but also made the first steps towards space travel; Lockheed's Constellation was a graceful and glamorous propeller airliner design, distinguished by its unusual triple tail design; Voyager I has travelled further than any other machine carrying Earth and mankind information, should it ever encounter another civilisation; She may have been humble in size, but the *SS Meredith Victory* deserves recognition for the scale of her humanitarian achievement; Big Muskie may have been massive, but that didn't stop this dragline being able to 'walk' – albeit rather slowly!

INTRODUCTION

Small machines are everywhere these days. Our modern world just couldn't function without the tiny devices that we now use everyday – in our homes, where we work, just out and about – as a matter of course. We take such items for granted. We hardly even think about them anymore. They're just there.

However, there are many machines around that simply can't be taken for granted, thanks to their sheer size and it is these mega machines that this book is about. From the past, through the present, to the future, this is a collection of the most enormous, the most powerful, the most brutal mechanical leviathans ever conceived.

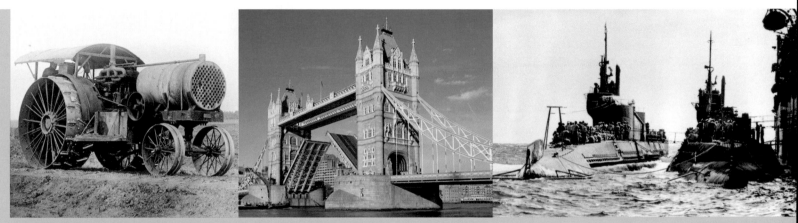

ABOVE: The Minneapolis Twin City 60-90 tractor built between World Wars I and II, weighed an incredible 12,700kg (28,000lbs); It may not seem a conventional machine but beneath the stonework, London's Tower Bridge is just a huge lifting device; As if the ability to attack unseen wasn't enough, Japanese Sen Toku submarines also carried aircraft, they were larger than any submarine ever seen.

BELOW: The 'Big Roy' 1080 eight-wheel drive tractor built in the 1970s was the biggest of its type ever built.

But these aren't just any old big machines however. They're the largest of their type, the superlatives of their breed, the most epic vehicles and equipment mankind has ever dreamt up. From the worlds of land, sea, air and space, this book is a celebration of the greatest gigantic machines throughout history, mobile and static feats of human engineering that go far beyond the normal, into the realms of the extreme.

Not all of the machines within this book exist any more, while others are just confined to museums these days. And many of the ones that are still in action are often rarely seen in public. However, if you do get the chance to see any of the giants featured here, hard at work as their makers intended, then do so. Words and pictures are no substitute for the fascinating and awe-inspiring real things…

CLOCKWISE: The unique and enormous 1974 Terex Titan gave new meaning to the phrase 'Monster Truck.'; Huge effort was required to make Yugi Gagarin the first human in space aboard Vostok I in 1961; More than 21,000 DUKWs were built during World War II – proving their worth in situations like this where river crossings were destroyed.

ABOVE: Although the style of the F-150 may have changed, its impressive load-lugging abilities remain constant.

BELOW: This photo of the RMS *Titanic* gives an idea of how huge she was…and thus what a disaster it was when she sunk in 1912; Some steam engines were epic: this Prescott pump is 18.9m (62ft) tall and weighs over 813,000kg (800 tons).

RIGHT: The wide, long tunnels of today are made easier by giant tunnel boring machines like 'Big Becky' here, the largest tunnel boring machine of all time; Superfortress by name and nature: the B-29 was the biggest, most advanced bomber of WWII.

THE LARGEST DUMP TRUCK (DIESEL ELECTRICAL)

LIEBHERR T 282B

Liebherr's massive T 282B dumper just edges out Caterpillar's 797 for the title of the largest truck in the world. So huge they can't be driven on roads, these trucks are confined to the world's great mining and engineering sites.

RIGHT: The four enormous tyres on the rear axle of the Liebherr T 282B help distribute the dumper body's payload weight, as well as provide good grip on rough surfaces.

SPECIFICATIONS

Country: Germany
Year built: 2004
Dimensions:
14.5m (47ft 6in) long;
7.3m (24ft) wide
Capacity: 400,000kg
(440 tons)
Maximum speed:
65km/h (40mph)
Power: 2.7mW
(3650bhp)
Cost: $3.5 million

The Liebherr T 282 truck appeared in 1998 as a German contender to the enormous material-carrying vehicles built by US manufacturers such as Caterpillar. However, it wasn't until 2004 that the range was refined and made larger still, with the resultant T 282B finally becoming the biggest truck on the planet.

As tall as three stories

The sheer size is staggering. They are as tall as a three-storey building, and only a few dozen are sold each year. They are made in a dedicated factory that covers the area of over seven US football fields but which can work on only four trucks at one time. The vehicles aren't completed here, but have to be finally completed at the worksite. And if they subsequently move anywhere else for another job, they have to be disassembled again.

What also makes the T 282B stand out from the rest of the dump-truck crowd is that instead of a diesel-mechanical drive system, its Detroit Diesel/MTU engine powers two electric motors on the rear axles, making it an AC diesel-electric truck – the first of its type to employ this supposedly more refined drive system. However, despite the multi-million dollar price tag of each T 282B, you still don't get a CD player or air conditioning as standard. These are both classed as optional extras!

CATERPILLAR 797B

The gigantic 797B has only recently been surpassed as the world's largest truck. However, it is still officially the biggest diesel-mechanical drive dumper around, and more than capable of taking on the toughest mining and engineering tasks.

Up until 2004 (and the advent of the Liebherr T 282B), Caterpillar's 797B off-road dumper was the hugest and most impressive of them all. However, when Liebherr's new behemoth came on the scene, it managed to surpass the 797B's load ability by 20,000kg (22 tons).

But never mind, because Caterpillar can still call the 797B the world's biggest diesel-mechanical drive dumper truck, in which the diesel engine directly powers the axles via a seven-speed transmission. The truck is used primarily for open-pit mining, and a full load in the dumper body is 380,000kg (418 tons), which happens to be 102,000kg (112 tons) more than the vehicle's own body weight. What limits the 797B from carrying more is simply tyre technology. Despite each tyre on the 797B weighing 4000kg (4.5 tons) and standing 9.7m (13ft) tall, they still have to be replaced every 56,327km (35,000 miles). Bigger weights would significantly reduce this interval.

A big power source is needed to move all this weight around, even if the top speed is a mere 67.7km/h (42mph). In fact, the Cat 3524B engine is actually made up of two 12-cylinder engines coupled together. This creates a 117.1 litre (7146 cu in) 24-cylinder turbocharged diesel unit, with a power output of 2647kW (3550bhp), fed by a tank with a capacity of 6814 litre (1800 gallon) fuel. Such features make it almost as much an impressive mega machine as the 797B it actually powers!

SPECIFICATIONS

Country: USA
Year built: 2002–date
Dimensions:
7.6m (25ft) long;
14.5m (47ft 6in) wide
Capacity: 345,000kg
(380 tons)
Weight: 252,000kg
(278 tons)
Maximum speed:
68km/h (42mph)
Cost: $5–6 million

BELOW AND RIGHT:
The Caterpillar off-highway truck is a gigantic vehicle. Comparison of two workers standing beside the 797B graphically illustrates this.

THE LARGEST WHEEL LOADER
(DIESEL-MECHANICAL DRIVE)

CATERPILLAR 994F

One of the few machines comparable to LeTorneau's L-2350 wheel loader is the Caterpillar 994F, which can boast of being the world's largest diesel-mechanical drive wheel loader, even if it isn't (quite) the largest overall.

LEFT AND ABOVE: Big dump trucks need big loaders to serve them, with enough reach to be able to quickly deposit loads for transportation.

SPECIFICATIONS

Country: USA
Year built: 2005–date
Dimensions:
19.5m (64ft) long;
7m (23ft) high
Weight: 195,434kg
(215 tons)
Power: 1176kW
(1577hp)
Bucket payload:
35,000kg (38.5 tons)
Cost: $7 million

According to some sources, Caterpillar's 994D is the largest wheel loader around. What is also certain is that it's one of the biggest machines that the American firm builds (and by far the biggest of its loaders), and is the largest wheel loader to feature mechanical drive. With this system, power from the 1176kW (1577hp) engine is supplied directly to all the wheels, not via an electric motor as with the vehicles like the L-2350. Despite the hefty engine output, the 994F is more about low-down grunt rather than sheer speed, so it is geared to have a top speed of just 24km/h (15mph).

Choice of buckets

So that the 994F proves useful in a number of different environments, it can be fitted with an extensive selection of buckets, the largest of which measures 6.3m (21ft) wide and can scoop up 35.9m³ (47 yards³). Such sizes are primarily intended for shifting coal, however, and the buckets for other mining and quarrying purposes are smaller, but tougher, in order to deal with the harder rocks the 994F is likely to encounter.

Up in the cab, the 994F is quite technologically advanced compared to its rivals. A single joystick is used for direction, gear selection and steering, rather than the several controls that once did all this. There's even a rear-view camera. However, a few basic creature comforts haven't been forgotten – the second (trainer) seat can fold down to be used as a drinks tray, and underneath it, there's space for a lunch cooler.

THE LARGEST TRACKED LOADER

CATERPILLAR 973C TRACKED LOADER

For really tough loading jobs on difficult terrain, only a tracked vehicle can tackle the challenge. This is where a machine like the Caterpillar 973C comes in, because it is capable of going places that a wheeled loader wouldn't dare to tread.

SPECIFICATIONS

Country: USA
Year built from: 1990s
Power: 178kW (242hp)
Dimensions: 5.2m (17ft) long (without bucket); 3m (9.2ft) wide (without bucket)
Weight: 26,373kg (29 tons)
Bucket capacity: 3.2m³ (4.19yards³)
Cost: Approximately $350,000

BELOW: Try doing this in a rubber-tyred wheel loader! Under difficult steel mill conditions like this, tracked loaders come into their element.

Wheeled loaders do have their limitations. On loose, rough or very muddy ground, they can get bogged down. In addition, landfill sites, where the piles of rubbish can provide a very difficult surface for normal tyres to get a grip, can be a challenge.

Better distribution and grip

Under such circumstances, a tracked loader is the obvious option instead. Because the tracks distribute the load and grip of the machine over a greater area, such loaders are more adept at working – even if they're not that manoeuvrable on 'normal' ground.

It is no wonder, then, that the Caterpillar Company (which is actually named after the tracks it bought the patents for at the turn of the twentieth century) should be at the forefront of tracked vehicles to this day. The 973C is its largest tracked loader. Looking rather like a bulldozer, the 973C, for all its bulk, can be quite a dexterous machine, thanks to its hydraulic arms that allow it to raise and lower its front bucket to a variety of different angles and positions. It can act as a grader, flattening soil into roads with some finesse, although it's also capable of churning it up with the assistance of the three big rippers on its rear. Other common usages are demolishing buildings and even shovelling hot materials in steel mills. The 973C is quite a 'Jekyll and Hyde' machine, but immensely practical and versatile because of all the different jobs it can carry out.

THE LARGEST COLD PLANER, CURRENT

ROADTEC RX-900 COLD PLANER

Once big highways and airport runways have been laid out, they need to be maintained and, every so often, resurfaced. Enter the RX-900 cold planer, a big machine for the biggest of repaving tasks.

SPECIFICATIONS

Country: USA
Year built from: 2004
Dimensions:
16.8m (55ft) long;
2.7m (9ft) wide
Weight: 37,195kg
(41 tons)
Maximum speed:
5.1km/h (3.2mph)
Power: 708.5kW
(950hp)
Cost: Upwards of
$550,000

ABOVE: A cold planer like the RX-900 is far quicker and more cost-effective than having men do the same job manually with drills.

However well built a road or runway is, the constant pounding of vehicles eventually takes its toll on its surface. That's when it's time to call in a cold planer. Such equipment is used to remove old concrete or asphalt so it can be repaired.

Cutting through road surfaces

Cold planers can be small (as used for repairing driveways), they can be large or, in the case of RoadTec's RX-900, they can be massive. Thanks to its highly powerful engines – the largest unit available is a 708.5kW (950hp) Caterpillar diesel engine – the RX-900 is able to exert enough force to cut down through a solid road surface to a depth of up to 355mm (14in) and to a maximum width of 3.81m (12ft 6in). It's not exactly quick about the task, with a maximum working speed of just 39m (128ft) per minute, but few other cold planers are so versatile. It certainly beats using men with pneumatic drills to do the same thing!

The RX-900 is available with four caterpillar tracks or just three (two at the front and one at the rear, which makes it look like an extremely strange back-to-front tricycle), but one of its more noticeable features is the covered conveyer belt that emerges from the front of the machine. Capable of swinging 60° to either side, the belt is almost 7m (23ft) long and is used to transfer the waste surface material into dump trucks that travel along with the cold planer.

THE LARGEST CABLE EXCAVATOR

P&H 5700 CABLE SHOVEL

Just five of the enormous P&H shovels were built, and not all of them managed to survive their employment intact. One of them ended up being titanic in more than sheer size alone.

S till regarded as the largest two-crawler shovels ever, P&H's 5700 series of excavators was conceived during a time of economic optimism. Unfortunately, by the time these giants were ready for production, economic recession meant that P&H had trouble finding customers. From 1978 to 1991, just five of these white elephants were built.

Electric marvels

Known as cable shovels because their power came from electricity supplied by large cables strung out behind them, the first 5700 weighed in at 1,610,253kg (1775 tons). But the breed grew larger still during its limited lifetime, with the final two machines tipping the scales at 1,905,088kg (2100 tons). Shovel capacity also varied, rising from 22.8m^3 (29.8 yards^3) to 52.6m^3 (68.8 yards^3).

Four of the machines were used for loading oversized dump trucks at mines in Australia and America, but the third one to be built was something of a curiosity. It ended up mounted on a large barge being used for dredging the Great Lakes off Illinois. However, the Chicago, as the 5700 was christened, came to an unfortunate end while being moved across the North Sea to Denmark. It was hit by a high wave, capsized and sank to the bottom of the ocean. And because a salvage operation to bring it up is regarded as simply too expensive, that's where it remains to this day.

BELOW: This was the fourth 5700 to be built, upgraded to XPA specification and employed at a mine in New South Wales, Australia.

SPECIFICATIONS	
Country: USA	
Year built from: 1978–1991	
Dimensions: N/A	
Weight: 1,905,088kg (2100 tons)	
Shovel Capacity: 52.6m^3 (68.8 yards^3)	
Boom Length: 27.4m (90ft)	
Cost: N/A	

TRENCOR 1260RS ROCK SAW

No, it's not just a trencher. The 1260RS made by Trencor of Texas is intended to be brought in for conditions that would defeat even the biggest and best conventional trenchers, because this machine is the world's largest rock saw.

The literature for Trencor's 1260RS insists 'It is NOT a converted chain trencher.' As good as modern trench cutters are, they sometimes have to give up. The Trencor's 1860HD is designed to cope with a certain amount of rock, but if large chunks break off, these can jam the mechanism and bring the machine to a halt.

Super saw

However, this amazing machine, which would seem quite at home appearing in a James Bond film, isn't likely to let a little bit of hard rock put it off its stroke. The lethal and scary-looking blade at the front likes nothing better than to slice through rock at a maximum speed of 21.8 revolutions per minute, either so cables can be laid in the resultant gap, or to soften up the ground for other trenchers to follow along afterwards.

Based on Caterpillar technology – both the diesel engine and the crawlers come from the bigger US company – the front blade is lowered into place hydraulically when the 1260RS begins work. Different types of saw wheel can be fitted, ranging from 11.5cm (8in) to 30.5cm (16in) and capable of digging down to a depth of 137cm (54in). The saw wheel can also be reversed, so instead of cutting while the tractor pushes, it does so while being pulled – a process that generally makes less of a mess with waste material.

SPECIFICATIONS

Country: USA
Year built: current
Dimensions:
10m (33ft) long;
3.2m (11ft) wide
Weight: 45,400kg
(50 tons)
Power: 392kW (525hp)
Cost: N/A

ABOVE: No rock is safe from the mean-looking Trencor 1260RS and its fearsome saw.

THE LARGEST PIPELAYER, PRODUCTION
CAT 589 PIPELAYER

After the ditching machines have done their job, it's time for the pipelayers to come in to lay pipes. Biggest of the current Caterpillar line-up is the 589, able to handle the biggest tubes with its heavy-duty winch and hook system.

BELOW: A Cat 589 makes light work of manoeuvring large sections of pipework into place.

Pipelayers like the Cat 589 don't usually work on their own. Intended for the bigger construction projects, they normally operate as part of a team, and the sight of several of these monsters lined up in a row, manoeuvring a continuous length of gas or oil pipe into place, rarely fails to impress.

As much as they look like little more than winches or small cranes, a purpose-built pipelayer is somewhat more complicated than this. The chief difference is the counterweight that is hydraulically extended out of the side when the pipelayer is in action, to improve load balance and clearance, and prevent the machine from toppling forwards.

Elevated drive sprockets

However, as the flagship of the Caterpillar pipelaying range, the 589 comes with certain features that you won't find with pipelayers from other manufacturers. The boom is longer than usual, at 7.3m (24ft), and can lift up to 103,330kg (113 tons). Down on the undercarriage, the main drive sprockets are elevated above the crawler wheels, so the tracks take on a triangular appearance. This helps protect them from damage from objects on the ground, as well as contribute further to the 589's balance.

But what the majority of operators will appreciate most of all is the provision of a fully enclosed cab – many pipelayers don't even have this. However, because the 589 often finds itself out in very inhospitable locations, such as Alaska, it has to offer good protection from the weather. There's even a cold-weather package as an optional extra. It also makes the 589 very distinctive in profile, in common with other Caterpillar machines that use this form of drive.

SPECIFICATIONS

Country:	USA
Year built from:	1990s
Dimensions:	length 5.9m (19ft 6in); width 6.7m (22ft)
Weight:	65,336kg (72 tons)
Max speed:	10.9km/h (6.8mph)
Power:	313kW (420hp)
Cost:	N/A

SPECIFICATIONS

Country: Denmark
Year built from: 1990s
Dimensions:
120m (394ft) high;
146.3m (480ft)
total diameter
Weight: 10,000,000kg
(11,023 tons)
Lifting weight:
108,862kg (120 tons)
Swing speed: 0.4
revolutions per minute
Cost: N/A

THE LARGEST TOWER CRANE (CONSTRUCTION)

KROLL K-10000 TOWER CRANE

As buildings get ever larger, so do the cranes that build them. The giant of them all, however, is the Kroll K-10000, which is almost as magnificent and towering a creation as the structure it helps to build.

Denmark may not be a country associated with soaring skyscrapers, but without a machine built by a Danish company, some of the world's tallest buildings would have been far more difficult to construct.

Kroll's K-10000 tower crane dwarfs other cranes. At 120m (394ft) tall, it's almost three times the size of the Statue of Liberty, which stands at 46m (151ft) high, and five times that of a conventional tower crane. In fact, it is so lofty that it has a smaller service crane mounted on top of the main frame so essential items can be hoisted up to it. Despite its stature, it can withstand winds of over 280km/h (174mph).

Everything about the Kroll-10000 seems larger than life. It's capable of lifting the objects the equivalent weight of two large military tanks. When it swings its 91m (300ft) boom, the diameter it covers is the size of six American football pitches.

Moving the K-10000

There are very few K-10000 cranes around, so when one is needed for a project, it will be shipped anywhere in the world. A recent job in Indiana, USA, saw the Kroll arrive on 320 separate truckloads. Because even the base takes up so much space and the crane has to be anchored in concrete, the Kroll is often placed directly in the centre of the construction site, and the structure built up around it. And what becomes of the hole that is left once the building is close to completion? That usually ends up as the main lift shaft.

THE LARGEST MOBILE CRANE

MAMMOET PLATFORM TWINRING CONTAINERIZED MOBILE CRANE

Perhaps it's only fitting that the Mammoet Platform Twinring Containerized mobile crane has such a long and convoluted name. It is, after all, the biggest mobile crane in the world, and not exactly used to going unnoticed.

Fortunately, the moniker of Mammoet's gigantic piece of lifting equipment can also be shortened to PTC, although 'Momo' is a nickname that is commonly used as well. When installation, repair or construction jobs are too heavy for a conventional trailer-mounted crane to deal with, the PTC comes into its own.

Although not a 'true' mobile crane insomuch as it arrives on site at jobs fully assembled and ready to work, the PTC's modular construction allows it to be easily packed away in standard shipping containers of 6m x 12m (20ft x 40ft) for relocation elsewhere. However, it does occupy 88 of those containers, and for one job in the USA in 2001, it turned up in 169 trucks.

Mounted on a huge ring supported by jacks, the latest PTC can lift up to 2,000,000kg (2204 tons). It has a 'superlift' mode allowing it to handle ultra-heavy weights whereby a ballast load is suspended from its boom support arm and hangs out over the rear of the crane. Under usual circumstances, this counterweight is normally hung within the circumference of the rotating ring.

ABOVE AND LEFT: The Mammoet needs a complicated system of booms and cables, plus a large counterweight for balance.

SPECIFICATIONS

Country: Netherlands
Year built from: 2000
Weight: 2,100,000kg (2315 tons)
Lifting weight: 2,000,000kg (2204 tons)
Lifting height: 200m (656ft)
Time to rotate through 360°: 8 minutes
Cost: N/A

THE LARGEST JET-PROPELLED CAR

THRUSTSSC

The world's largest jet-powered car isn't the obvious record that comes to mind with ThrustSSC. This was, after all, the car that broke the land speed record and also became the first vehicle to travel faster than the speed of sound on the ground.

BELOW: The two enormous General Electric J79-GE-17A jet engines dwarf the rest of the bodywork. With two wheels at the back and one at the front, ThrustSSC can also lay claim to being the world's fastest three-wheeler.

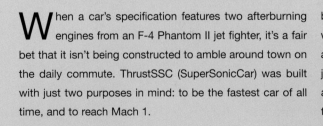

W hen a car's specification features two afterburning engines from an F-4 Phantom II jet fighter, it's a fair bet that it isn't being constructed to amble around town on the daily commute. ThrustSSC (SuperSonicCar) was built with just two purposes in mind: to be the fastest car of all time, and to reach Mach 1.

Up against America

The brainchild of Richard Noble – who had taken the land speed record in 1983 with Thrust2 – ThrustSCC was put together between 1994 and 1996, and taken to the Black Rock Desert in Nevada, USA, for the speed attempt in 1997. It had competition from a US rival, *Spirit of America*, but repeated engine problems for the US car meant that it was ThrustSSC, driven by RAF pilot Andy Green, that was able to achieve Mach 1.016 or 1227.99km/h (763.035mph), just one day after the fiftieth anniversary of Chuck Yeager achieving the same thing in the air. An extraordinary photo taken of the run showed the sonic shockwave spreading out from ThrustSSC as it achieved Mach speed – something that had never been photographed before.

ThrustSSC now resides in a museum in Coventry, in the UK, where its 16.5m (54ft) length and 3.7m (12ft) width, along with its 4.73m (15ft 6in) long engines, can be appreciated up close – even if the Thrust's ability to reach 1000km/h (600mph) in just 16 seconds can't.

SPECIFICATIONS

Country: UK
Year built: 1994–1996
Dimensions:
16.5m (54ft) long;
3.7m (12ft) wide
Weight: 10,500kg
(11.5 tons)
Maximum speed:
Mach 1.016/
1227.99km/h
(763.035mph)
Thrust: 223kN
(50,000lb) from two
engines
Fuel consumption:
5500 litres per 100km
(0.04 mpg)
Cost: N/A

SPECIFICATIONS

Country: Germany

Year built from: 1999

Dimensions: 4.5m (14.6ft) long; 2m (6 6ft) wide

Weight: 1888kg (4162lb)

Maximum speed: 407km/h (253mph)

Acceleration: 0–96.5 km/h (60mph) in 2.7 seconds

Power: 775.5kW (1040hp)

Cost: $1,440,880

THE LARGEST ENGINE CAPACITY, CURRENT PRODUCTION

BUGATTI VEYRON

When Volkswagen revitalized the famous Bugatti racing marque in 1999, it was the Veyron sportscar that made all the headlines. It's the most powerful, expensive and fast car currently available, which would make it enough of a true mega machine even if it didn't also have the world's largest capacity engine.

TOP AND ABOVE:
Whether at rest or in motion, the Veyron looks spectacular.

It's taken a long time for the Bugatti Veyron to reach production, although with a mere 70 or so cars built during 2006, production isn't quite the word. The world's most exclusive sportscar was seen at various car shows and events across the world for seven years before building models for customers started properly in 2006.

Speedy but thirsty

Still, there's little about this car that is like anything else on the roads. Top speed of the Veyron is an almost unbelievable 407km/h (253mph), although it could go faster if current tyre technology would allow it. At those kind of speeds, though, it manages a fuel consumption of 125 litres per 100km (2.1 miles per gallon), which is enough to empty the petrol tank in a mere 12.5 minutes.

At the heart of this road-going rocket is a W16 engine of 7993cc (488ci), the biggest engine by capacity of any car built today. The design is essentially two V8 engines mated together, with a total power output of a rather impressive 775.5kW (1040hp).

The current price for the Bugatti is around $1,440,880. Still, it's even more expensive for Volkswagen, as it has been estimated that each car costs the German car firm over $9,250,000 to make.

SPECIFICATIONS

Country: France
Year built: 1929–1933
Dimensions:
6.5m (21ft) long;
4m (14ft) wheelbase
Weight: 3175kg
(7000lb)
Speed: N/A
Power: 12,763cc
(779cu in
Number built:
6, plus 1 prototype
Cost: Fr500,000 for
basic chassis

ABOVE AND BELOW:
Nothing discreet about a
Bugatti Royale – a car
designed to impress! At
the top is a Napoleon
Coupe de Ville version
while the bottom car has
coachwork by Binder.
Note the elephant
mascot that adorns
all Royales.

THE LARGEST CAR OF ALL TIME

BUGATTI ROYALE

**There has never been a more extravagant car than
a Bugatti Royale, or a bigger one. These huge
French cars were the last words in elegance and
power, intended to surpass Rolls-Royces and
Cadillacs as the ultimate luxury road machine.
Although the intention was only to make 25,
only six were built.**

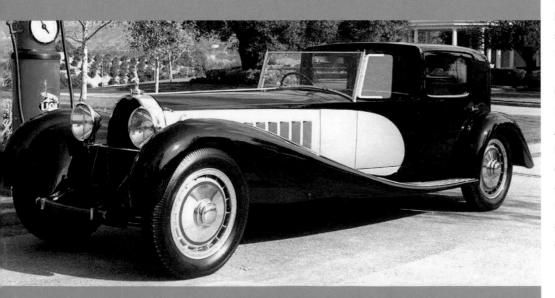

The radiator mascot of the Bugatti Royale
was an elephant, somewhat fitting for a
car that was larger than anything else and,
ultimately, one of motoring's biggest white
elephants. After an Englishman told Ettore
Bugatti that 'If one desired to be fastest, one
must choose a Bugatti, but it was evident that
if one wanted the best, one must choose a
Rolls-Royce,' Bugatti vowed to come up with
something that would change this.

Grand scale

And the massive Type 41 Royale was just such
a car. It was first seen as a prototype at the
German Grand Prix in 1928, and everything
about it was to a grand scale. An extensive
bonnet housed a 12,763cc (779cu in) engine of
around 224kW (300hp), and the rest of the
bodywork was built to the same epic scale,
with overall length stretching to over 6m (20ft).
Every one of the further six built had a different
body, ranging from low, sleek roadster to very
stately limousine, the latter intended for
European royalty.

Competition

Unfortunately, there was a competitor from
America in the shape of the almost as grand,
but cheaper, Duesenberg, and many of the
customers intended for the Bugatti bought one
of these instead. It was a blow to Ettore
Bugatti's pride, and production was halted,
although the powerful engine design later went
on to be used in French railcars.

THE WIDEST CAR OF ALL TIME

KOENIG COMPETITION

BELOW: The Koenig Competition was based on the Ferrari Testarossa, but tuned to perfection and sporting a body kit to make it even more visually exciting. Coupe and convertible versions are illustrated.

Koenig is a German tuning firm that started tuning Ferraris in 1974. Its most successful model was the Koenig Competition, based on the 1980s Ferrari Testarossa. Among the changes carried out were broader body kits and bigger wheels, thus creating the widest car in the world.

When Ferrari unleashed its Testarossa in 1984, it was a stunner. With a 4942cc (301.5 cu in) 12-cylinder engine and a top speed of 291km/h (181mph), there was little else around at the time to compare for performance and handling. Its distinctive side cooling slats also made it into the widest production car around, at 1.97m (6ft 6in).

Powering up

For those who just wanted a bit more than Ferrari could offer, Koenig had its extreme Competition tuning package. Among the options wealthy customers could select were a 745kW (1000hp) twin turbo engine – enough to send the car rocketing up to 370km/h (230mph) – plus brake and suspension modifications so the driver could keep control at that kind of speed.

To make the Koenig-modified Testarossa even more special, these mechanical changes could be accompanied by new body kits, and a convertible version. It was the front and rear wing extensions, made of carbon-kevlar or glass fibre, that bulked the Koenig Competition out to almost 2.2m (7.2ft), an increase of 22cm (8.7in) over the standard Ferrari, and by far the broadest car in the world. Of course, all this did mean that you also needed a very wide road to enjoy a Koenig Competition.

SPECIFICATIONS

Country: Italy (built), Germany (modified)

Year built: 1984–1992

Dimensions:
4.5m (14ft 6in) long;
2.2m (7ft) wide

Weight: 1589kg (3500lb)

Maximum speed: 370km/h (230mph)

Power: 745.5kW (1000hp)

Engine displacement: 4942cc (301.5 cu in)

Cost: $94,000 for standard Testarossa (1985 price)

DUESENBERG SJ

Duesenberg was one of the most glamorous of all American car marques, rivalling European firms like Rolls-Royce and Bugatti for exclusivity and luxury. Its greatest model was the SJ, a supercharged version of the already very special (and expensive) Model J. These cars became the longest cars – bar limousines – ever built.

Introduced in 1928, the Duesenberg Model J was a no-expense-spared attempt to build the best car in the world. And, with customized bodywork coming from the best coachbuilders in Europe and America, several of the cars undoubtedly were the greatest of their kind. But such luxury came at considerable cost. At launch, the top model cost $25,000, the equivalent of almost $360,000, or over eight times the annual salary of a doctor of the era.

Supercharging arrives

But there was more to come. In 1932 came a supercharged version of the J, dubbed the SJ. Sheer power, 235.5kW (320hp), and speed, 217–225km/h (135–140mph),

were just two of the features that made this type particularly stand out, but some of the body styles customers could choose were the longest ever on a non-stretched production model. For example, the SJ Town Car stretched a vast 6.25m (20ft 6in).

Unfortunately for Duesenberg, the price and opulence of its cars made it very vulnerable to economic conditions, and the financial depression throughout the 1930s meant that it was rarely far away from going out of business. In 1937, the inevitable happened, and Duesenberg, along with sister car firms Cord and Auburn, collapsed. Some of the most fantastic American cars ever, were suddenly no more.

SPECIFICATIONS

for SJ Town Car
Country: USA
Year built: 1932–1937
Dimensions:
6.25m (20ft 6in) long;
1.88m (6ft) wide
Weight: 2905kg
(6400lb)
Maximum speed:
170km/h (106mph)
Engine displacement:
6884cc (420cu in)
supercharged
Power: 238kW (320hp)
Cost: $9500 for basic chassis

THE LARGEST TOUR COACH

DESERT STORM TOUR BUS

Based on a standard American school bus, the coach known as Desert Storm, used on tours around the sand dunes north of Perth in Western Australia, now has little in common with its educational-use sisters. Converted to four-wheel drive and running on huge tyres to allow it to negotiate the dunes, it's claimed by its owners to be the largest 4x4 tour bus in the world.

ABOVE: It may be a bus used to school runs, but military style suspension and heavy duty off-road tyres mean Desert Storm is now happy to tackle loose sand dunes.

The idea to run adventure trips so that tourists could explore the 4km (1.5 mile) square area of desert and dunes around Lancelin in Western Australia was envisaged in 1997, but an immediate barrier was the lack of a suitable vehicle. There was nothing capable of taking passengers over loose sand hills sometimes up to 50m (164ft) in length.

Monster truck tour bus

So, the tour company decided to have its own made. A standard 32-seat school bus was shipped over from America, but a few changes were carried out. Heavy-duty military specification suspension and four-wheel-drive mechanics were fitted, with the whole ensemble topped off by four 'Monster Truck' type tyres to give Desert Storm a height of 4m (13 ft) – the usual height for this kind of vehicle is about 3m (10ft 6in). The lower bodywork was extended downwards to cover up the running gear, but Desert Storm still has superb ground clearance. And to emphasize the contrast between it and a standard school bus, the traditional yellow livery was retained. Desert Storm has Terra 1.7m (5ft 6in) tall tyres, four-wheel steering and a 1000-watt sound system!

THE LARGEST BICYCLE EVER

DIDI SENFT BICYCLE

Didi Senft is one of life's eccentrics – a passionate German cycling enthusiast who turns up at every Tour de France dressed as a devil, just for the fun of it. However, he's also an inventor, who has created over 100 cycles, one of which is listed by the *Guinness Book of Records* as the biggest on the planet.

LEFT AND BELOW: Didi Senft's bike is so tall, it has trouble fitting through bridges and tunnels.

SPECIFICATIONS

Country: Germany
Year built: N/A
Dimensions: 8m (25ft 6in) long; 4m (12ft) tall
Weight: N/A
Power: One person power
Cost: N/A

If you're ever watching the Tour de France and a very cheerful Satan with a German accent pops up beside you brandishing a pitchfork, don't be too concerned. It's likely to be Didi Senft, and somewhere nearby will probably be one of the largest bicycles in the world. For most events that Didi attends, he tows a huge bike behind his van.

Beyond an ordinary bike

However, this cycle isn't the largest in the world. That one stays behind when Didi is on the road, because it's so tall that, he says, he has trouble transporting it under bridges and through mountain tunnels. Which isn't really much of a surprise because it is 8m (25ft 6in) long and

4m (12ft) tall. The wheels alone measure over 3m (10ft) tall. Despite being twice the size of an average person, the bike can be ridden, although it does require a few helpful people around to hold it up while the rider gets on. Braking and getting off again can also be a little tricky too.

Bicycle chain

The mechanism of the aluminium-framed bike is conventional (and the same size as you'd find on an ordinary-sized version), but the chain has to go through some complicated linkages to make it able to reach the back wheels and still be linked to pedals that can be used by the rider.

THE LARGEST MOTORCYCLE EVER

GREG DUNHAM MOTORCYCLE

RIGHT AND BELOW:
You can see just how large Greg Dunham's motorcycle is when it is compared with a car and a truck.

When friends of Gregory Dunham bet him he wouldn't be able to build the world's largest rideable motorcycle, he told them he could. Of course, it did take three years of work and cost him about $300,000 to do so. But at least he made it into the *Guinness Book of Records*.

Most people probably wouldn't take a bet to build the biggest operational motorcycle on the planet that seriously. After all, when Greg Dunham's friends made the wager, there was a massive motorbike already in existence. Called Big Toe and powered by a 5343cc (326cu in) Jaguar V12 engine, it had been finished in Sweden in 1998 and measured 2m (8 ft) high by 5m (15ft) long. If Dunham really wanted to beat that record, he'd have to build something pretty incredible.

Stepping on the Big Toe

However, he managed it. Despite the three-year timescale and the substantial amount of money, by 2005, Dunham had constructed something that eclipsed even Big Toe – in most dimensions. His motorbike was over a 1m (3ft) taller and nearly 1.5m (5ft) longer. Its tyres alone – at 2m (6ft) – were almost as big as Big Toe was high in its entirety, and at 8.2 litres (502cu in), the engines were more substantial.

Safety features

Because the 'proper' handlebars are in scale with the rest of the bike, the actual steering (plus the other controls) is from a small cage mounted below this part of the bike. And, although ostensibly a two-wheeled machine, this most grown-up of bikes does need small stabilizers on the rear wheels, to stop it falling over.

SPECIFICATIONS

Country: USA
Years built: 2003–2005
Dimensions: 6m (25ft) long; 3m (11ft) tall
Weight: 2950kg (3 tons)
Engine size: 8.2l (502cu in)
Maximum speed: N/A
Cost: $300,000

THE LARGEST PRODUCTION TRUCK, CURRENT

INTERNATIONAL CXT PICK-UP TRUCK

The letters stand for Commercial Extreme Truck. International's CXT is the largest pick-up truck in the world, making even a Hummer look like a compact car by comparison. However, it's far from being a working pick-up, for this flashy flatbed is aimed firmly at the wealthy and well known.

This definitely isn't the sort of pick-up truck you'll find down at your local building site – certainly not at $115,000 a pop! If anything, the four-wheel-drive CXT has invented a new niche for itself – that of the celebrity luxury load lugger, just the kind of thing for bringing multiple Oscars or gold records back from awards ceremonies.

Big on luxury

Based on International's rugged dump trucks and snow ploughs, it is twice the weight of a Hummer H2 and stands 2.7m (9ft) tall; little about it is subtle. The stated gross vehicle weight of 11,792.9kg (11.7 tons) is carefully calculated – for anything over 11,793.4kg (13 tons) means it could be bought only with a commercial trucker's licence. Goodies inside include a DVD player, satellite navigation, rear camera, tinted windows, lots of leather and a very loud sound system. Outside, there's an excess of chrome for extra effect. Production is limited to only between 500 and 1000 a year.

Naturally, the engine is also big, a diesel V8 putting out up to 224kW (300hp) from its 'MaxxForce' diesel engine – enough to allow the CXT to tow 18,144 kg (20 tons) and carry 4989 kg (5.5 tons) in its load bay. However, the penalty for all this size and power is that fuel consumption can drop as low as 4.3–6.2km per 3.79 litres (7–10 miles per gallon).

Country: USA

Years built from: 2004

Dimensions: 6.4m (21ft) long; 3m (9ft) wide

Weight (loaded): 11,792kg (13 tons)

Maximum speed: Approximately 129km/h (80mph)

Power: 224kW (300hp)

Cost: $115,000

FAR LEFT, LEFT AND ABOVE: The CXT looks more big rig than normal road pick-up – in fact, it's based on a dump truck!

'BIG BOY' STEAM LOCOMOTIVE

Some steam locomotives have been heavier. Some steam locomotives have been more powerful. But no mainstream steam locomotive has ever been larger than the 'Big Boy' engines built by the USA's Union Pacific Railroad in the 1940s to pull its heaviest freight trains over mountain passes.

Only 25 'Big Boys' (as the UP's 4000 class 4-8-8-4 locos have been so aptly nicknamed) were built between 1941 and 1944. Yet they have become one of the best known railway engines of all time, thanks to their sheer size and the awe-inspiring sight they made when working hard. Although austere in appearance, there was also a strange grace and beauty to their tremendous strength.

Mountain beaters

They were constructed to be able to pull long, high-speed goods trains, weighing up to 3,300,000kg (3640 tons), over the Wasatch Mountains in the American Midwest. Previously, helper locomotives had been needed because the gradients were so steep. The delays had been slowing down service times as well as causing extra expense, but the 'Big Boys' soon eradicated these. Massively powerful, but also very fast for an articulated freight loco (speeds of 130km/h [80mph] were possible), the Big Boys soon earned a fine reputation, not just for their load-lugging abilities but also for being easy to drive, despite their mass.

The rapid dieselization and electrification of the US railway system meant that all the 'Big Boys' were withdrawn from service by 1959, years before the end of their useful life. However, they were still among the last steamers to continue running in regular service in America. Eight have been preserved, although none are operational. One problem with restoring one to working order is that there is simply nowhere to run it.

TOP AND ABOVE : The main driving wheels of a 'Big Boy' were on bogies, to allow the enormous locomotives to negotiate corners. Even with these, they were still too large for most UP routes.

SPECIFICATIONS

Country: USA

Years built:
1941–1944

Dimensions: 40.5m
(133ft) long

Weight: 548,279kg
(604 tons)

Maximum speed:
130km/h (80mph)

Power: 4698kW
(6300hp)

Tractive effort:
602.18kN (135,375lbf)

Cost: N/A

THE LARGEST DIESEL LOCOMOTIVE, EVER

UNION PACIFIC CENTENNIAL DDA40X DIESEL LOCO

The Union Pacific's reputation for using massive locomotives continued beyond the Big Boy steam era, and into the diesel epoch. Its DDA40X class of freight locomotives, purchased to do exactly the same sort of duties carried out decades earlier by the Big Boys, were the largest and most powerful diesel-electric types ever built.

I t was on 10 May 1869 that a golden spike was driven to mark the completion of the USA's first transcontinental railroad. One hundred years later, one of the companies involved, Union Pacific, celebrated the anniversary by taking delivery of the first of its colossal Centennial class of diesel locomotives, also known, rather less memorably, as the DDA40X series. (The 'X' stood for experimental, as EMD intended studying them as working testbeds for new technology). The first locomotive was numbered 6900 to commemorate the events of '69.

Twin diesel power

The Electro-Motive division of General Motors built 47 of these distinctive yellow machines between 1969 and 1971, and nothing else around was bigger or more powerful. Weighing almost 250,000kg (275 tons) and measuring 30m (98ft 6in) in length, total power output was 4900kW (6600hp), albeit generated by two V16 engines. Paralleling the careers of Big Boy and Challenger, they were withdrawn well before their time, in 1980, as a result of an economic downturn. In 1984, 25 were returned to service, but by 1986 they were all gone for good from regular service. Thirteen have been preserved, one (No 6936) by Union Pacific itself, which uses it for special excursions.

SPECIFICATIONS	
Country: USA	
Years built: 1969–1971	
Dimensions: 30m (98ft 6in) long; 3m (10ft 6in) wide	
Weight: 247,400 kg (273 tons)	
Maximum speed: 145km/h (90mph)	
Power: 4900kW (6600hp)	
Tractive effort: 605kN (136,000lbf)	
Cost: N/A	

BELOW: Side view illustrates the vast size of the Centennial diesel loco.

THE LARGEST PASSENGER TRAIN, REGULAR SERVICE

AMTRAK AUTO TRAIN

ABOVE AND BELOW: Double decker Superliner passenger coaches and car carriers give the Auto Train a lot of capacity, yet a typical train is still about 40 cars long.

The question of the longest passenger train in regular service in the world is a contentious one. Many cite the Eurostar sets between London, Paris and Brussels as the holders of the record, with their 18 carriages and two power cars stretching 394m (1293ft). However, Amtrak's Auto Train in the USA also has a good claim to the fame.

SPECIFICATIONS

Country: USA	
Years built from: 1971	
Length: Approximately 0.8km (0.5 mile)	
Wagons: Approximately 40	
Weight: N/A	
Maximum speed: 177km/h (110mph) P42DC Genesis locomotive	
Average speed: 83.6km/h (52mph)	
Total power: 6000kW (8000hp) from two locomotives	
Cost: N/A	

Unlike Eurostar, the Auto Train, which runs the 1376km (855 miles) between Lorton (near Washington DC) and Sanford, Florida, isn't a pure passenger train. It also has vehicle-carrying wagons, known as autoracks, allowing passengers to bring their cars and vans with them. The passenger coaches and autoracks combined add up to the longest train of its type currently in operation.

Long train coming

Operating nonstop (except for one fuelling and crew change) between its terminals, the first Auto Train ran in 1971, with a typical setup comprising between 30 and 64 coaches and wagons, pulled by up to three locomotives. Amtrak took over in 1983 after the original company went bankrupt. A typical train is now formed of two General Electric P42 Genesis diesel-electric locomotives and around 40 railcars, depending on demand, with the usual length of a train about 0.8km (0.5 mile). Because the service operates overnight, sleeping cars are also included in the formation, something else that contributes to making an Auto Train so long.

Operating every day, with trains at both ends leaving at 4pm and arriving the following morning at 8am, it has been estimated that 200,000 passengers opt to let the Auto Train take the strain rather than drive on the congested highways between the north eastern seaboard of the United States and the popular holiday destination of Florida.

THE LARGEST TANK, CURRENT (BY WEIGHT)

CHALLENGER II
MAIN BATTLE TANK

Typical of the modern breed of enormous main battle tanks, the Challenger II is very large, very heavy and very deadly. Mainstay of the British Army, it is also used by the Royal Army of Oman, and has seen action in the major conflicts of recent years, including the last Gulf War.

ABOVE AND BELOW: The Challenger II is designed to fight around the world, in any conditions, under any circumstances.

Although it uses the same hull and much of the same mechanical equipment as the earlier Challenger I tank (introduced in 1982), the Challenger II of 1994 is resolutely a tank for the 21st century. Equipped with the latest in weaponry and target-finding equipment, it is one of the most advanced – and potent – armoured fighting machines around today, as well as being the heaviest.

Heavy weapon, heavy armour

Its main armament is a 120mm (4.7in) rifled gun, designed to take out other tanks, vehicles and buildings. Also fitted are a chain machine gun and an anti-aircraft gun. Computer and digital systems are included to make the weapons more effective, as are a laser rangefinder and night vision.

Very tough Chobham armour is intended to provide protection against all kinds of attack, including chemical, nuclear and biological.

Time for tea

The Challenger II is crewed by four personnel, with power coming from a 12-cylinder Rolls-Royce Perkins diesel engine. Combined with Hydragas suspension (a system using fluid and air, and found, in somewhat smaller form, on several popular British cars such as the Austin Allegro, Princess and Metro from the 1970s onwards), this allows the Challenger II a comparatively high top speed of 60km/h (37mph). Being a British vehicle, one of its most essential pieces of equipment is the water boiler, used to make tea.

SPECIFICATIONS

Country: UK

Year built from: 1994

Dimensions: 8m (27ft) long; 3.5m (11ft 6in) wide

Weight: 62,500kg (69 tons)

Maximum speed: 60km/h (37mph)

Power: 894.8kw (1200hp)

Cost: Approx $1.2 billion

THE LARGEST TANK EVER BUILT

PANZERKAMPF WAGEN (PZKPFW) MAUS SUPER-HEAVY TANK

The ironically named Maus (mouse) wasn't just the largest and heaviest tank to be built during World War II, it remains the biggest tank ever constructed. However, by the time it was ready to go into production, Germany was on the verge of defeat, and only two prototypes were completed.

ABOVE: The first Maus undergoing tests, with a dummy turret fitted. Ultimately, just two prototypes were built, both proving to be quite useless.

Described as 'this gigantic offspring of the fantasy of Hitler and his advisers', the Maus was more a propaganda weapon than a useful fighting machine. It would have done the Nazi war effort no harm at all if it were to be made known that the country possessed the largest and most powerful tank in the world. But in reality, the Maus was too expensive, too heavy, too slow and too complicated.

Mammoth to mouse

Originally known as the Mammut (Mammoth), the inappropriately titled Maus was designed by Ferdinand Porsche, the man responsible for the Volkswagen Beetle and whose son would go on to build Porsche sportscars. The first prototype was completed by the end of 1943 – albeit with a mocked-up, non-functional turret – and a second followed in 1944, this time fully operational.

Too heavy

Fitted with a huge 128mm (5in) gun, the Maus had armour that was 240mm (9in) thick in places. This pushed the weight up to a staggering 191,000kg (210 tons) – too heavy for the V12 petrol-engined tank to manoeuvre effectively or have any useful speed. It was too heavy for most bridges too, so a snorkel device was incorporated to allow it to go under water to a depth of 13m (45ft).

Both versions of this behemoth of a tank were damaged in combat and captured by the Soviets, who made them into one complete vehicle, which is still on display at the Russian Tank Museum.

SPECIFICATIONS
Country: Germany
Years built: 1943–1944
Dimensions: 11m (33ft); 4m (12 ft) long
Weight: 191,000kg (210 tons)
Maximum speed: 20km/h (12mph)
Power: 783kw (1080hp)
Cost: N/A

THE LARGEST GUN EVER

SCHWERER GUSTAV BIG GUN

Epic and deadly in equal measure, the German Schwerer Gustav 80cm (31.5in) railway gun of World War II was the biggest artillery weapon to have been both built and fired in anger. However, during its four-year life, it fired just 78 shots under battle conditions, before being deliberately sabotaged to stop it falling into Allied hands.

BELOW: So big was the Schwerer Gustav that it had to run on two parallel railway lines, specially built at its firing position. Range was 38km (23.5 miles).

The original reasoning behind the Schwerer Gustav big gun, conceived in 1934, was that it was to be used by the Germans to destroy concrete fortresses on the French Maginot defensive line, in the event of any future German invasion. It was a massive undertaking – the calculation calling for an artillery piece that could fire a 7000kg (8 ton) shell from long range beyond the reach of enemy weapons, with the barrel over 30m (98ft) long and weighing well over 1,000,000kg (1102 tons). The final gun would be so large that it would need to be transported by rail.

Mobile WMD

But, by the time this mobile weapon of mass destruction was finally complete, in 1942, France had already fallen. So the Schwerer Gustav went to Russia instead. The train that carried all of its equipment was 25 wagons long, stretching 1.6km (1 mile). Deployed against the besieged city of Sevastopol, the gun required 200 men and three days to be reassembled, with new railway track having to be laid by some 2500 men to get it into suitable firing positions. The 48 rounds fired, from 5 to 17 June, caused great damage, and Sevastopol fell on 4 July.

A proposed attack against Leningrad was cancelled, and, as the war turned and the Germans started to retreat in 1944, the gun came with them, firing 30 rounds into the Warsaw Ghetto during the 1944 uprising. It was destroyed in early 1945 to prevent its capture.

SPECIFICATIONS

Country: Germany
Years built: 1941–1942
Dimensions: 47m (155ft) long; 7m (23ft) wide; 12m (38ft) tall
Weight: 1,350,000kg (1490 tons)
Total power: 1382kW (1853hp) from two diesel locomotives
Barrel length: 32.5m (107ft)
Price: N/A

ABOVE: The MT900B's size makes articulation practically a necessity – with steering being done by the back wheels rather than the front.

THE LARGEST FOUR-WHEEL DRIVE TRACTOR

CHALLENGER MT900B

The Challenger range also encompasses 'conventional' wheeled tractors. 'Conventional' is probably not quite the right word to describe something as imposing as this agricultural monster with four chunky tyres to each axle.

SPECIFICATIONS

Country: USA
Year built from: 2006
Power: 425kW (570hp)
Max speed: 40km/h (25mph)
Weight: 27,000kg (30 tons)
Dimensions: 7.6m (25ft) long; 5m (17ft) wide
Cost: N/A

Fancy something of the size and power of Challenger's MT800B range of tractors, but would prefer it to have wheels instead of tracks? The MT900B series is practically the equivalent of the big tracked Challengers, except that it is fitted with wheels in each corner instead.

All-wheel drive, rear-wheel steer

There are four MT900B tractors, with the MT975B undoubtedly the flagship of the range, thanks to its Caterpillar turbocharged C18 ACERT diesel engine, which delivers a not inconsiderable 425kW (570hp). However, despite the resemblance to the tracked '800s, the '900s are more than just the same machines with tyres instead of tracks. The chief difference (apart from slightly increased dimensions and the obvious

eight stocky tyres, with two on each hub) is that the tractors are articulated behind the cab. This makes them more manoeuvrable than they would be with a rigid frame. Unusually, though, it's the back wheels that do the steering – the front ones stay fixed, parallel to the front bodywork. However, with all the wheels powered, having the rear ones doing the turning makes the tractors more versatile because they can achieve a tighter turning circle.

There's one aspect of the M900B that puts one over on its tracked stablemates, and that's speed. The maximum speed that one of these is capable of is 40km/h (25mph). Maybe that's not much by usual vehicle standards, but over a muddy ploughed field while towing a scraper or a harrow, that's a pretty outstanding pace.

THE LARGEST ROW-CROP TRACTOR

JOHN DEERE 8530 ROW-CROP TRACTOR

A row-crop tractor is a machine that typically has an adjustable tread width and a higher ground clearance than other tractors. This enables it to work in fields planted with tall crops planted in rows. Typical of the biggest of this type is John Deere's 8530 model.

The original John Deere was born in 1804 in Vermont, USA. He was a blacksmith by trade but moved in to making agricultural machinery. The company he founded remains one of the oldest in America, and is much respected in the agricultural world. Vehicles like the 8530 are only likely to further enhance that reputation.

It isn't just the size of the John Deere 8530 that makes it so notable. It's the power as well. By their nature, row-crop tractors have to be more delicate than other agricultural machines because they need to be able to make their way accurately and carefully down lines of crops, doing as little damage as possible. However, the 8530 still manages to be muscular and mighty, without compromising those needs. At 205kW (275hp), it is the most powerful row-crop tractor ever built.

Narrow and tall

The chief features of the 8530 are its narrow bodywork, needed to negotiate crop passageways (though the double rows of tyres do increase the total width significantly), as well as the tall cab, dubbed the Command View by John Deere. The cab comes complete with a computer display allowing the operator to monitor all aspects of what the tractor is doing, and how well it's doing it. What isn't obvious from looking is the innovative gearbox, known as Infinitely Variable Transmission (IVT), which allows smooth gear changes without the need for a clutch.

SPECIFICATIONS

Country:	USA
Year built from:	2005
Power:	205kW (275hp)
Maximum speed:	42km/h (26mph)
Weight:	11,400kg (12.5 tons)
Dimensions:	N/A
Cost:	$216,265

BELOW AND RIGHT: The John Deere 8530 can be fitted with two tyres to each wheel for when those farming jobs get tough. Narrow body and high ground clearance allows the 8530 to pass over crops without damaging them.

THE LARGEST COTTON PICKER

JOHN DEERE 9996 COTTON PICKER

Once upon a time, labourers used to harvest a crop of cotton by hand. That changed from the 1950s onwards, with the gradual introduction of the cotton picker, a machine that can work more than one row at a time. In fact, one machine can accomplish the equivalent of what once took up to 240 people to achieve.

Looking almost like a mutated vacuum cleaner, the John Deere 9996 is a common sight around the cotton states of the USA. This substantially built and complicated-looking machine travels down a row of plants, and removes cotton lint and seed, and is able to do up to six rows simultaneously. It achieves this using barbed spindles that rotate at high speed and separate the seed-cotton. The seed-cotton is then passed through to a basket, where eventually a 'brick' of cotton is created, which can be easily stored back at the main farm.

Four-wheel drive to eight tyres

The 9996 is among the elite of cotton pickers. The ability to pick six rows at once makes it stand out as a highly productive tool, and with its six-cylinder turbocharged diesel engine rated at 261kW (350hp), there's little to compare with it in terms of sheer power. Four-wheel drive (and two tyres on every axle hub as standard) gives it the ability to tackle rough ground, and its large-capacity basket of 427m³ (15,069 ft³) allows the machine to keep harvesting after many other rival machines have to stop and be emptied.

The console allows smooth fingertip control, and easy speed control. The basket is monitored electronically, so when it is full, a light come on the cab and a horn sounds for three seconds – unmistakeable signals, no matter how wrapped up the driver is in his work.

ABOVE AND RIGHT: Forward-mounted, high-positioned cab gives the 9996 operator excellent visibility while working. Picked seed is stored in the cage at the back.

SPECIFICATIONS

Country: USA
Year built: current
Dimensions: 8.5m (28ft) long; 5m (17ft 6in) tall
Weight: 20,400kg (22.5 tons)
Max speed: 19km/h (12mph)
Power: 261kW (350hp)
Cost: $430,000

ABOVE: Wide cutting
blade makes harvesting
a snip – the 590-R can
gather 8m (26ft).

THE LARGEST COMBINE HARVESTER

CLAAS LEXION 590-R COMBINE HARVESTER

The largest machines found on most farms are combine harvesters. So a combine harvester that's bigger than any of the others has to be something pretty amazing – an appropriate description indeed for the mega machine that is the Lexion 590-R.

The Lexion 590-R, and its sister machine, the 595-R, are two of the biggest machines in agriculture. Not only are the two machines the largest combine harvesters ever built, but they're also the most powerful as well. The difference between the two is that the 590-R has wheels, while the 595-R has tracks at the front and wheels at the rear.

Installed in front of the Lexions are headers, a set of removable cutters that are interchangeable depending on the crop. The combine harvester travels through the field, threshing the crop and passing it through the throat of the machine where the seed is separated. The seed passes through a chute on to a truck running by the side of the harvester, leaving the hay as a separate by-product.

Power, size and technology

A few features make the 590/595-Rs stand out from the others. The 385kW (516hp) of power it wields is not an inconsiderable amount for any vehicle. Its size is substantial too, with the largest header measuring a full 8m (26ft) across. The technology inside is almost like something from a computer-game console. Driving speed and direction are controlled by a joystick, which is also used to adjust the cutter height, start and stop the loading process, and even activate the autopilot. Yes, there really is an autopilot – these machines are that advanced. They are definitely masters in their field.

THE LARGEST TELEHANDLER

TH580B TELEHANDLER

It's a close-fought thing between Caterpillar's TH580B and JLG's G12-55A machines in the battle for telehandler supremacy. The JLG may have more power and be able to carry more, but the Caterpillar is bigger and can reach just that little bit higher.

Telehander is actually a contraction of 'telescopic handler' and is one of the more widely used machines in large-scale agriculture. Essentially, it's a more versatile forklift truck, with a telescopic boom instead of a sliding lift mechanism, which means it can stretch forwards as well as upwards. Different attachments can be fitted to the end of the arm, and the handler has the ability to traverse tougher terrain than a forklift would be able to manage, thanks to its chunky tyres.

Long and far

One of the undisputed kings of the type is Caterpillar's TH580B, which has a quite astonishing height and reach. It can lift objects up to 17m (56ft) above the ground, and its boom can stretch out up to 13m (42ft) away from the vehicle. However, this practicality comes at a cost: the more the TH580B extends its arm, the less it can carry, as the boom acts as a giant lever and makes it unstable, even with hydraulic jacks extended. Maximum capacity is a not inconsiderable 5000kg (11,000lb), but at maximum lift height, it can manage only around 2500kg (5500lb). It's even more 'puny' at full reach, when just 1333kg (2500lb) is the max – and that's with stabilizers. Nevertheless, these kind of weights are still well beyond the vast majority of other telehandlers. Most of the lifting operations are done through one very versatile joystick, down by the righthand side of the driver. It also has three different steering modes: two wheel, crab and circle steer. All it takes to toggle between them is just a single, three position switch.

SPECIFICATIONS

Country: USA
Year built from: 2003
Dimensions:
6.6m (21.73ft) long;
2.54m (8ft 3in) wide
Maximum speed:
40kph (25mph)
Maximum reach:
17m (56 ft)
Maximum weight:
5000kg (11,000lb)
Price: $125,000

THE LARGEST PLANTER

JOHN DEERE DB90 PLANTER

BELOW: The yellow box in the centre of the DB90 is the 'Central Commodity System' – the hopper that holds the seeds for distribution to the 36 trailing arms.

The most important agricultural job is to grow things, and that process starts with the planting. As with almost everything else in the world of farming, the job isn't just fully mechanized now, but has its own mega machines.

Once upon a time, planting was done by hand, by scattering the seeds on ploughed land. Not any more, though. To get the highest crop yields, and to plant the fields in neat little rows that other machines can negotiate when the plants are growing, is now a highly precise job.

Extra wide for extra productivity

These days, the job calls for something like the John Deere DB90 planter, one of the latest generations of extra-wide planters and capable of seeding an area 27.5m (90ft) wide in one go as it is towed behind a tractor. When being transported between jobs, however, the planter can be folded up into five sections, reducing its size to a mere 5.36m (17ft 6in).

Spread out over its breadth, the DB90 has 36 rows, each one finishing in a seed dispenser. Fed by a main central hopper and with electrical power provided via the tractor, these dispensers distribute seeds in a flow regulated by the operator. Naturally, of course, it's all high-tech, with electronic systems monitoring every aspect of the seeding process. Powerful springs keep each row as close to the soil as possible so as not to waste any seed, and the flexible frame means the whole apparatus bends with the lie of the land. So, if a field isn't flat, then it is no problem, because as wide as it is, the DB90 can still cope.

KALMAR LMV 88 FORKLIFT TRUCKS

Forklift trucks are small and agile, and primarily intended to carry only small loads so they don't fall over. That's usually the case, except for the three trucks built by Kalmar back in 1991, which were anything but diminutive.

SPECIFICATIONS	
Country: Sweden	
Year built: 1991	
Dimensions: N/A	
Power: N/A	
Maximum lifting weight: 79,832kg (88 tons)	
Maximum lifting height: 2.4m (7ft 6in)	
Cost: N/A	

Today, the largest forklift truck made by Swedish firm Kalmar can lift 45,360kg (50 tons), while another has a tall enough lifting arm to allow it to stack a modern shipping container on top of four others. Either of these machines are worthy enough to earn Kalmar a place in this book.

Record still unsurpassed

However, these achievements pale into insignificance compared to the three trucks that Kalmar built back in 1991. The company was specially commissioned to build machines that were capable of lifting a staggering 176,000kg (195 tons), which is still something unsurpassed by any other maker. It was also enough to earn Kalmar a place in the *Guinness Book of Records*.

Built for an industrial concern, these diesel-engined, rubber-tyred heavy lifters were able to achieve this feat by being very long and counterbalanced with ballast at their rear. This meant that the weight of what they were carrying was balanced by the vehicle's own rear mass. However, despite this design, the loading height was somewhat limited, with the forks only able to raise objects up to 2.5m (7ft 6in). Anything beyond this, and the trucks would have been in serious danger of becoming unstable and pitching forward.

Since these incredible Kalmar vehicles were made, nobody else has managed to construct a forklift that has the same impressive level of lifting ability – or even comes close to it.

ABOVE: Industrial forklift trucks can cope with different shapes – the tilting arm and prongs allow this Kalmar to carry pipework without it rolling off.

THE LARGEST LOG SKIDDER/FORWARDER

TRANS-GESCO TG88D LOG SKIDDER

Log skidder? Sounds complicated. What modern log skidders do is exactly the same thing that teams of horses and mules used to do in centuries gone past – they literally drag felled trees through a forest using sheer brute force, so they can be loaded onto trucks or trains.

TOP AND ABOVE:
Crawler tracks and
a hefty engine
allow the TG88D to
successfully manoeuvre
and drag logs.

Suffice to say, such a job requires a lot of grip and power, something a machine like Trans-Gesco's imposing TG88D log skidder is able to offer by the bucket load. This tracked 298kW (400hp) turbocharged diesel-powered beast is the planet's largest skidder and forwarder. It is fitted with a 4.2m² (45ft²) grapple that is able to cope with the larger and longer trees that typically grow in North America. The boom that the grapple is mounted on can reach out as far as 8m (26ft).

SPECIFICATIONS

Country: Canada
Date built: Current
Dimensions: N/A
Capacity: 31,750kg
(35 tons)
Power: 298kW (400hp)
Price: N/A

When the going gets rough

The TG88D has three variants: the grapple skidder (fitted with, as its name suggests, a big grapple); a clambunk skidder (which has a different attachment where timber can be gradually loaded instead of grasped all at once as a grapple does); and a forwarder (which carries the logs clear of the ground on a trailer, in order to avoid damage to trees and soil, although this does limit the size of the timber that can be moved). The forwarder can cope with a payload of 22,700kg (25 tons), while the others can manage 31,750kg (35 tons), but the grapple skidder offers the further benefit of being able to use its hydraulic boom (normally folded out of the way when travelling, to aid the TG88D's balance) to push itself along if the ground gets too rough.

THE LARGEST LAWNMOWER

CLAAS COUGAR

Lawn mowers are traditionally quite compact – even the ones you sit on. Not so the Claas Cougar. This is a machine so large that its main problem is finding somewhere with enough grass for it to cut.

ABOVE: Retractable arms spread out from the Claas Cougar to allow it to cut areas much wider than the vehicle's breadth.

You won't find too many of these in the average suburban garden, trimming the lawn on a Sunday. The Claas Cougar mower is the big boy of the mowing world, a 350kW (480hp) monster that can clear up to 20 hectares (50 acres) an hour under ideal conditions.

From wide to narrow

The Cougar bristles with five limbs, to which grass-cutting attachments can be fixed. Full control from the cab allows these to be manipulated into any position to manoeuvre them around obstacles, or fold them out of the way completely. This is just as well because, with the Cougar being able to cut at widths of 14m (46ft), it needs a big area to play with. However, with the arms folded up, the whole machine shrinks to just 3.5m (11ft) wide.

Its top speed is 24km/h (15mph) while cutting, or 40km/h (25mph) when just travelling between jobs. One of the Cougar's more novel features is that its cab can be rotated through 180°. When the machine is working, it faces the blades. When just driving normally, it points the other way, so the lethal cutting edges are safely tucked away at the rear. For this reason, the four-wheel drive machine also has all-wheel steering as well, so that it handles (more or less) in the same way, whichever direction it is being driven in. When you're in something with this many sharp edges, accidents really aren't advisable!

AL JON INC VANTAGE 600 COMPACTOR

Today's landfill sites need specialist machines to squash all the waste of modern life, and not much surpasses Al Jon's Vantage 600 when it comes to rolling rubbish. The Al Jon Vantage is simply the biggest compactor money can buy.

Why compact trash? Well, law regulates most landfills, so they are allowed to reach only a certain height. And, if nothing else, a huge pile of rubbish is hardly the most attractive of sights.

Traditionally, bulldozers have been the usual machines to work on landfill sites, but because their load is spread out, they don't do a great job of actually compressing what's below them. Compactors, though, are specialized machines intended specifically to pile down waste.

Weight, size and power

Weight is the key to success, which puts the Vantage 600 right at the top of its league. At 57,000kg (63 tons), it is heavier than any of its rivals, as well as being larger and more powerful. Trundling along on menacing looking spikes, a hydrostatic transmission applies constant torque to the wheels, meaning it has superb adhesion and the ability to change direction without losing power. A blade of more than 5m (17ft) wide at the front allows the 600 to push heaped rubbish over so it can drive on top of it, and the operator hasn't been forgotten, either. In order to combat the, let us say, 'fragrance' of a landfill site, the cab is fitted with a system that filters fresh air from outside to make the job a little less smelly. There's also a rear-view camera with a monitor, just in case the driver wants to check if a bit has been missed.

SPECIFICATIONS

Country: USA
Year built: Current
Power: 447.5 kW (600hp)
Maximum speed: 8kph (5mph)
Weight: 57,000 kg (63 tons)
Dimensions: 9.6m (31ft 6in) long; 4.7m (15ft 6in) wide
Cost: Approx $500,000

TOP RIGHT AND BELOW: It may not be pretty – but with that blade and those heavy spiked wheels, the Vantage 600 gets the job done.

THE LARGEST SAIL WARSHIP, EVER

VALMY, 1847

In the nineteenth century, gaining supremacy of the seas was one of the main concerns of the major European nations. An advantage in the oceans meant profitable colonies, profitable trade routes and international standing. And although it was the British Royal Navy that ultimately 'rules the waves', it was the French who built the largest sailed warship ever.

ABOVE: This painting depicts the *Valmy* in 1867, by which time she had been renamed the *Borda*.

SPECIFICATIONS

Country: France
Year built: 1836–1847
Dimensions:
64m (210ft) long;
18m (59ft) wide
Weight: 5,826,000kg
(6422 tons)
Speed: N/A
Number of guns: 120
Cost: N/A

Size was everything in the 1800s, and in 1847 when the French Navy launched the *Valmy,* named after a battle fought during the French Revolution, she seemed to prove this point. She was the largest warship in the world, and would remain so until the British matched her with the HMS *Duke of Wellington* six years later. However, that ship, although starting as a sailing ship, was converted to steam power while being constructed. That meant that the *Valmy* remained the largest warship powered by the wind, and still does, to this day. In fact, it was actually thought impossible at the time that a sail warship could be built bigger, because the extensive rigging required on anything larger would be too complex to be operated just by manpower alone.

Steam supersedes sail

But it also meant she was obsolete very quickly, lacking the new technology of the era, namely, steam engines. Her size – three decks, each loaded with guns – didn't make her that easy to manoeuvre either. The only time she went into battle, during the bombardment of Sevastapol in the Crimean War, she actually had to be towed by a newer steam warship.

Despite being less than 10 years old, she was deemed past her usefulness by 1855, and became a training ship and renamed. She was scrapped in 1891, at the age of 44. But for only eight of those years had she actually served as a warship, the purpose for which she was built. Perhaps, in the case of the *Valmy,* size wasn't everything.

THE LARGEST PADDLE STEAM SHIP, CURRENT

AMERICAN QUEEN

Although steam power has now been largely superseded as a means of motive power for the world's largest ships, there are still many steam-driven ships operating all over the world, and giving faithful service. The largest of these is the *American Queen,* a modern recreation of the classic Mississippi riverboat.

SPECIFICATIONS

Country: USA

Year built: 1995

Dimensions:
127m (418ft) long;
27m (89ft) wide

Weight: 3,362,935kg
(3707 tons)

Speed: 18km/h
(9.5 knots/11mph)

**Number of
passengers:** 436, plus
160 crew

Cost: $60 million

The *American Queen,* operated by the Delta Queen Steamboat Company around the wide rivers of America's Deep South, is not all that she seems. Although she looks decades old, she was actually launched in 1995, as a faithful replica of an historic Victorian riverboat. And although the enormous 8.5m (28ft) paddle at the stern is operated by steam power, it receives a little bit of a helping hand from two propellers mounted on either side of the wheel. These are powered by diesel, and actually provide most of the propulsion when she's underway.

Modern technology, Victorian style

In order to improve the *American Queen's* handling, the propellers are mounted in pods on the hull, and can be turned to change direction, using a system known as Z-drive. They can even face forwards, to cancel out forward motion if the *American Queen* has to be stopped in a hurry.

There are several other concessions that have been made to the modern world on board the six-deck steamer, which towers 30m (97ft 6in) above the river (although the smokestacks can be lowered for obstructions). Decorated outside with lacy filigree and inside with authentic Victorian opulence, her cabins still contain plenty of wood and antiques but retain all the mod cons that discerning customers would expect to find on most ships of today, including two lifts that are made necessary by her height. She can carry 436 passengers, along with a crew of 160.

ABOVE AND BELOW: Because the USA's inland rivers are so calm, riverboat decks can extend almost down to the waterline.

THE LARGEST SAIL-POWERED CLIPPER
CUTTY SARK

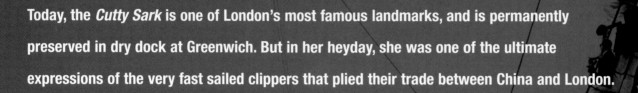

RIGHT AND BELOW: The central mast of the *Cutty Sark* – 19.8 m (65 ft) tall – gave her a graceful appearance. Here, the ship is being presented to the Thames Nautical Training College in 1938.

Today, the *Cutty Sark* is one of London's most famous landmarks, and is permanently preserved in dry dock at Greenwich. But in her heyday, she was one of the ultimate expressions of the very fast sailed clippers that plied their trade between China and London.

The *Cutty Sark* was what was known as a clipper, which was a highly manoeuvrable, very quick cargo ship distinguished by many masts and large sail areas for extra speed. One of the last to be built, she was born into a world where the steamship was becoming ever more dominant. She would spend just eight years performing her intended role as a tea carrier, during which time she did made only eight trips. She found fame in 1872 when racing another clipper back to London with the first tea of the season. Although she didn't win, thanks to losing her rudder en route, it was her captain's decision to press on using improvised steering that made her a maritime star.

Steam supplants sail

When steamships ousted the *Cutty Sark* from the tea routes in 1878, she went in to general service between Britain and Australia. On one journey, she managed to complete the trip in 67 days, which was extremely fast for the time, even by steamship standards. Her long-distance ocean travels came to an end in 1922, when she was restored and used as a training ship. She went into dry dock in Greenwich in 1954, as part of the National Maritime Museum's collection. Thousands of visitors visit the *Cutty Sark* every year and a major regeneration programme has just begun to ensure that the vessel continues to survive.

SPECIFICATIONS

Country: UK
Year built: 1869
Dimensions:
65m (212ft 6in) long;
11m (36ft) wide
Weight: 978,000kg
(1080 tons)
Speed: N/A
Crew: 70
Cost: £16,150

THOMAS W. LAWSON

Schooners (ships with at least two fore- and aft-rigged masts) were some of the few cargo sailing ships able to compete with steamboats in the later years of the nineteenth and the first years of the twentieth centuries. The culmination of their 300 years of development resulted in the enormous but beautiful *Thomas W. Lawson*, the only seven-masted sailing ship ever constructed.

SPECIFICATIONS

Country: USA
Year built: 1902
Dimensions:
117m (385ft) long;
11m (50ft) wide
Weight: 5,302,000kg
(5850 tons)
Speed: N/A
Crew: 16
Cost: £258,000

Built in 1902 for a Boston, Massachusetts, shipping company, the steel-hulled *Thomas W. Lawson* was one of the last-gasp efforts to build a freight craft that could compare in both size and speed to the latest steam-powered vessels. Her seven masts towered to a height of 58m (190ft) and she must have made a stirring sight with all of her sails hoisted. Two steam winches performed this operation, meaning that she could operate with a crew of just 16. Her total sail area was 4000m² (43,000ft²), and, because of their number, the crew christened her masts after the days of the week.

Lost at sea

Ironically, her original purpose was to transport coal, the very fuel that made her rivals go. However, her 11,177,000kg (12,320-ton) capacity and her sheer size proved too big for many loading ports, and she was converted into an oil tanker in 1906. However, she didn't last long at this job either, for tragic reasons. In December 1907, on her first transatlantic trip, she sank off the Scilly Isles with the loss of all her crew, save for her captain and one other. Nothing like her was ever built again.

RIGHT AND ABOVE: The seven masts were named after days of the week. The graceful appearance quite belied the ship's role as a coal and oil carrier.

THE LARGEST SUBMARINE, EVER

OSCAR II CLASS SUBMARINE SERIES

Although the largest attack submarines ever built, Russia's secretive Oscar II vessels might have gone unnoticed by the world in general had it not been for a tragic accident. In 2000, one of their members, the *Kursk,* was lost with all hands, despite an international rescue attempt.

The first Oscar submarines were constructed in the early 1980s, but it was their ultimate development into the Oscar II class later on in that decade that took them into the record books, surpassing the American Ohio-class subs. Regarded as unsinkable, thanks to their double hulls, they were also longer, heavier and able to dive deeper – down to 600m (1968ft) – than their predecessors. But a lot of information on these nuclear-powered and missile-equipped machines remains sketchy. The West learnt more about their construction, though, in the catastrophe that claimed the sixth out of the 10 Oscars IIs to be launched.

Tragedy at sea

In August 2000, during a training exercise, two huge explosions, the second so large it measured 4.4 on the Richter scale, sank the *Kursk.* The accident made the headlines around the world, as did the Russian, British and Norwegian attempts to rescue the 116 members of the crew, 108m (354ft) down. The efforts were in vain and unfortunately there were no survivors. The cause of the incident was later on blamed on a faulty torpedo.

Kursk's other nine sisters remain in service to this day.

SPECIFICATIONS

Country: Russia
Year built: 1986–1991
Dimensions:
155m (508ft) long;
18m (60ft) wide
Total weight:
16,400,000kg
(18,077 tons)
Speed: 59 km/h
(32 knots/37mph)
Power: 73,078.5kW
(98,000hp) from two
nuclear reactors
Crew: 48 officers, 68
personnel
Cost: N/A

TOP AND ABOVE: The size of the Oscar II series is partly down to the double hulls, one inside the other, to give better survivability in an attack.

SS-N-20 (R39) SUBMARINE-LAUNCHED BALLISTIC MISSILE

Few weapons of mass destruction are as terrifying as a submarine-launched nuclear missile. There's no warning and little chance of destroying the launcher before it fires, as there might be with a land-based site. One of the most frightening of all – because of its size – was the SS N-20 intercontinental ballistic missile (ICBM).

LEFT: An R39 out of its natural Typhoon submarine environment. The tip could carry ten nuclear warheads.

SPECIFICATIONS

Country: USSR/Russia
Years built: 1979–1989
Dimensions: 16m (52ft 6in) long; 2.4m (8ft) diameter
Payload: 2550kg (5622lb)
Total weight: 90,000kg (99 tons)
Speed: 'Hypersonic'
Range: 8250km (13,277 miles)
Cost: N/A

You can breathe a small sigh of relief. This deadly-looking missile – known in Russia as the R39 and in the West as the SS-N-20 Sturgeon – is no longer in use. Introduced in 1983 aboard the USSR's Typhoon Class of submarines, which were then the largest submarines in operation, the last of these weapons was taken out of service in 2004 after the submarines they were used on were scrapped as well.

Five times the speed of sound

Firing differed from a ground-based missile, with the SS-N-20 ejected from the submarine using a gas generator so as not to damage the vessel. Once it broke the surface of the water, the conventional rockets came into play, and the weapon operated like a conventional three-stage booster. Travelling at hypersonic speeds (five times the speed of

sound) and with each one having a yield of 200 kilotons, the potential if used against an enemy was deadly, especially as there would be absolutely no defence against them.

Capacity for destruction

Each SS-N-20 could carry 10 nuclear warheads, and each Typhoon could carry 20 of these in total. During the peak usage of these missiles, 120 were deployed on Russian vessels, which meant a total of 1200 warheads. From 1996, the missiles started to be taken out of service as a result of the terms of arms treaties. There were plans to create an even more potent successor, but so many prototypes failed during testing (submarine-launched ICBMs are more complicated than their traditional land counterparts) that the project was dropped.

THE LARGEST CONTAINER SHIP, CURRENT

EMMA MAERSK

With the largest ship ever built – the *Knock Nevis* supertanker – now serving as a static storage facility, the *Emma Maersk* has become the largest container ship in the world and the biggest oceangoing vessel still in current use. Yet she has a crew of only 13.

Compared to most of the other ships in this book, the *Emma Maersk* is a baby in age – she was launched in August of 2006. But she's hardly a baby in size. She is 398m (1305ft) long, so if she were to be laid upright beside the Empire State Building, she'd still be 16m (52.5ft) taller.

A load of containers

Named after the wife of the former CEO of the AP Moller-Maersk Group, which owns her, the *Emma Maersk* is able to transport 11,000 standard 6m (20ft) shipping containers. However, that figure is the estimation of Moller-Maersk, but others put the total capacity of the ship at closer to 14,500 TEU (twenty-foot equivalent units). When fully loaded, the containers on the deck stretch 22 across, and seven high, although there's room for an eighth layer if needed.

Such a ship obviously needs a big engine, and in the case of the *Emma Maersk,* she has the largest diesel engine ever manufactured. The 14-cylinder engine puts out around 80,080kW (107,389hp), and supplementary engines give an extra 53,641kW (40,000hp) for other ship functions. Usual speed should be around 25 knots, but it's likely that the ship will have a top speed considerably in excess of this. However, for commercial reasons, Moller-Maersk hasn't let on what it is.

The *Emma Maersk* has already been involved in one incident. While being built, a welding fire destroyed all her accommodation quarters, including the bridge. This added seven weeks onto her build time.

SPECIFICATIONS

Country: Denmark

Years built: 2005–2006

Dimensions: 398m (1305ft) long; 56m (185ft) wide

Total weight: 170,974,000kg (188,500 tons)

Speed: In excess of 47.2 km/h (25.5 knots/29mph)

Containers: Estimated 14,500

Crew: 13

Cost: $145 million

ABOVE: *Emma Maersk* in port. How many containers she can carry is a commercial secret, but 14,500 seems a reasonable estimate.

THE LARGEST OPEN DECK TRANSPORT SHIP (USED FOR CARRYING OTHER SHIPS)

BLUE MARLIN

Think of the *Blue Marlin* as an aquatic pick-up truck, and you won't be too far off the truth. This totally extraordinary vessel is semi-submersible, so its centre section can be lowered beneath the water to allow loading of heavy floating items, often many times larger than itself.

SPECIFICATIONS

Country: Norway (built), Netherlands (owned)
Year built: 2000
Dimensions: 225m (736ft 6in) long; 63m (207ft) wide
Deadweight: 76,061,000kg (84,000 tons)
Cruising speed: 27km/h (14.5 knots/ 17mph)
Power: 23,640kW (31,942hp)
Crew: Up to 55
Cost: Under £500 million, including modifications

Ships don't come much more amazing than the *Blue Marlin.* The largest heavy-lift transport ship in the world is almost a cross between a submarine and a dry-bulk carrier, with a long, flat, wide centre section. The term 'flo/flo' (for float on, float off) has been coined to describe the way this type of vessel works. Ballast tanks can be flooded to allow this 'bed' to submerge, allowing anything from cargo to drilling rigs and even whole ships to be floated on to it. The ballast tanks are then pumped out, and the ship rises and sets off to carry its load to its destination.

Getting bigger, getting better

When built, the *Marlin* had a load capacity of 27,215,542kg (30,000 tons), but work carried out from 2003 to 2004 increased her deck width and carrying abilities. Soon afterwards, she transported the oil platform, *Thunder Horse*, to Texas. That itself weighed 54,431,084kg (60,000 tons), so the modifications on her were obviously a total success.

However, the job that most caught the world's attention was when the *Blue Marlin* was hired by the US Navy to piggy-back the crippled USS *Cole* from the Yemen back to the United States after it was attacked by bombers. It was also responsible for moving the huge sea-based X-Band Radar for the US Government in 2006.

TOP AND ABOVE:
The MV *Blue Marlin* has transported the X-Band Radar as well as the damaged USS *Cole* warship.

THE LARGEST PIPE LAYER

PIPE LAYER
SOLITAIRE

Oceans are now no longer any barrier to major pipelines, thanks to ships like the *Solitaire*, a highly specialized pipe-laying vessel operated by the Swiss-based Allseas Group. Effectively a floating factory – where steel pipes are welded to together before being laid out – the *Solitaire* is an extraordinary example of man's maritime ingenuity.

BELOW: *Solitaire* in action, with its pipe-laying cradle lowered beneath the surface of the sea by cables.

The Allseas Group operates a fleet of six highly specialized ships built for its business of offshore pipe layinging and subsea construction. Pride of the fleet, though, is the *Solitaire,* the biggest pipelaying vessel in the world, and a machine that is astonishing to look at, with its cranes, front boom and helicopter landing pad.

How she works

At the aft of the *Solitaire* is a huge gantry – known as a stinger – from which the pipeline is gradually lowered to the bottom of the ocean. An automatic welding system onboard the vessel allows the ship to work at a fast rate. In the past, up to 9km (5.6 miles) have been achieved in one day using it. Thanks to her size and storage capacity, the *Solitaire* can carry up to 22,000,000kg (24,250 tons) of pipe, which allows her to operate far out in the ocean without having to return to port to replenish her stock or be supplied from support ships. Given the, often difficult, conditions in which these ships operate, this puts her at an advantage over her contemporaries.

A big ship should have some big achievements, and one such feat that the *Solitaire* has notched up is the deep-water laying record, having managed to place a pipeline at a depth of 2775m (9100ft).

SPECIFICATIONS	
Country: Switzerland	
Year built: 1998	
Dimensions: 397m (1302ft) long	
Total weight: 75,684,000kg (104,560 tons)	
Speed: 24km/h (13 knots/15mph)	
Pipe diameters: from 5cm (2in) to 152.4cm (60in)	
Crew: Up to 420	
Cost: N/A	

THE LARGEST MOBILE, FLOATING RADAR

SEA-BASED X-BAND RADAR

Looking like some kind of bizarre oil platform, the US Government's Sea-based X-Band Radar is one of the more unusual – and gigantic – floating structures. It serves as part of America's ballistic missile defence system, and is thought to be able to detect objects as small as a baseball from 4667km (2900 miles) away.

ABOVE AND BELOW: Despite its oil rig resemblance, the X-Band Radar can move under its own power, although for longer trips, a transporter ship like the *Blue Marlin* is quicker.

SPECIFICATIONS

Country: USA
Year built: 2002
Dimensions: 116m (380ft) long; 85m (280ft) tall
Weight: 49,895,161kg (55,000 tons)
Speed: Classified
Power: Classified
Crew: Up to 75
Cost: $900 million

Standing on an Russian-built semi-submersible oil-drilling platform, the United States' most unusual device for detecting incoming missiles isn't normally seen by the public. Based off a remote island in Alaska, but able to patrol the Pacific in its search for possible incoming attacks against the United States, the Sea-Based X-Band Radar rarely comes close to populated areas. However, in 2006 it was carried from Texas to Pearl Harbor around South America (because it was too large to fit through the Panama Canal) on the back of the *Blue Marlin* heavy transport ship. When it arrived in Hawaii, large crowds turned out to see it.

Classified capabilities

It may be the last they see of the X-Band Radar for quite some time. Designed to be totally self-contained, the floating installation has living quarters, workspaces, storage, power generators and a bridge and control room on its main deck. It is be crewed by 75 personnel. It has its own propulsion system, although quite what speed the ungainly machine can manage is classified. It isn't likely to be fast, though.

The main feature of the vessel, is the X-Band radome, which weighs 1,645,633kg (1814 tons) and requires over a megawatt of power to operate.

THE LARGEST ICEBREAKER
SS *MANHATTAN*

The story of the SS *Manhattan* is an intriguing one. Built as an oil tanker, she was fitted out as an icebreaker to see if it was viable for a ship to bring oil from the ice-laden Alaskan oil fields rather than build a pipeline. The fascinating adventure was not without incident.

The SS *Manhattan* was already the biggest and most powerful of all US commercial vessels when it was decided to use her for an experimental voyage in 1969. The ship – as long as the Empire State Building is tall – was cut into four pieces. It was then put back together again but heavily reinforced, with a new heavy-duty ice-breaking bow at her front. It made her the biggest icebreaker in the world by at least 15 times.

Trapped in ice

She set off from Pennsylvania for the Northwest Passage – the sea route connecting the Atlantic and the Pacific via the top of Canada – in August 1969, and encountered her first ice in September. At first, she was fine, managing to crack floes up to 18m (60ft) thick. However, as the ice got thicker, the challenges became tougher, and she became stuck. She was able to escape only when steam used for heating was diverted to her engines, adding an extra 5220kW (7000hp) to her 32,06kW (43,000hp) turbines. A Canadian icebreaker and a US Coastguard ship also assisted. After she had been extricated from the ice, she changed course and managed to reach the Prudhoe Bay Oil Field, where she took on a single token barrel of oil before returning to New York. The trial had proved that navigation by ship was still too difficult to attempt, and the Trans-Alaska pipeline was constructed instead.

ABOVE AND RIGHT: These pictures illustrate the type of arctic conditions the *Manhattan* was pitched against during its epic journey north.

THE LARGEST FLOATING HOTEL

RMS *QUEEN MARY*

The RMS *Queen Mary* is one of the most famous of the glamorous transatlantic liners introduced before World War II. In service until 1967, she went on to a second career as the world's biggest floating hotel, moored at Long Beach, California.

ABOVE: Old and new meet: in the foreground is the original *Queen Mary*, while the newly launched *Queen Mary 2* sails in behind. The two great liners exchanged whistles in salute.

SPECIFICATIONS

Country: UK	
Years built: 1930–1934, modified into hotel 1967–1972	
Dimensions: 311m (1,019ft 6in) long; 36m (118ft) wide	
Capacity: 1957 passengers plus 1174 crew	
Weight: 73,700,000kg (81,240 tons)	
Cruising speed: 55km/h (28.5 knots/ 33mph)	
Power: 119,312kW (160,000hp)	
Number of hotel rooms: 365	
Cost: £5 million	

The career of the *Queen Mary* has been anything but dull. Her maiden voyage took place in 1936, when she proved to be the fastest ship to cross the Atlantic. During the war, she was a troop ship. She was so prized by the Germans that a reward of $250,000 was offered to any U-boat commander who could sink her. After the conflict ended, she went back to being a UK–USA liner again.

From ship to building

When withdrawn from service in 1967, she sailed to Long Beach, California, where conversion work started to turn her into a hotel and museum. Most of her machinery was removed, and the interior completely revamped to turn her into luxury accommodation. Although she superficially retains her original looks, there is very little that hasn't been touched or altered in some way, and she is now classed by the Coastguard authorities as a building instead of a ship, because she is incapable of moving under her own power.

According to popular superstition, several ghosts haunt the *Queen Mary,* and the sound of splashing has been heard from the first-class pool, despite the fact that it has been drained for years. As one of the last remaining icons from the golden age of transatlantic sea travel, the *Queen Mary* has also featured in many films and television programmes, including doubling for the SS *Titanic*.

THE LARGEST LINER/CRUISE SHIP, EVER

RMS *QUEEN MARY 2*

A worthy successor to her illustrious Cunard Queen predecessors, such as the original *Queen Mary* and the *Queen Elizabeth,* the *Queen Mary 2* was the longest, tallest, widest passenger ship ever when launched in 2003. Although since superseded in tonnage by the cruise ship *Freedom of the Seas,* she still retains the laurels of being the biggest transatlantic ocean liner.

BELOW: The RMS *Queen Mary 2* is the largest of all the Cunard Queens.

What's one of the last things you'd expect to find on board an ocean liner? How about a planetarium? Well, the *Queen Mary 2* has one, in addition to her 15 restaurants and bars, five swimming pools, casino and ballroom. She also has many other modern amenities and entertainments that mark her out as probably the world's premier liner.

Not to be beaten

Conceived in 1998, the *Queen Mary 2* was always intended to be the most impressive passenger ship in the world. Indeed, when it was found out that bigger ships were planned for construction soon after completion, her design was enlarged simply so she could beat them.

Around 20,000 people were involved in her construction, which resulted in just nine months between her keel being laid and her launch. In January 2004, she was named by Queen Elizabeth II of Great Britain. During one cruise in 2006, she passed by her spiritual mother, the first *Queen Mary*, in Long Beach, California, and, in a poignant moment, the two exchanged whistle salutes.

The dual diesel/gas turbine-powered *QM2* has already joined the ranks of her glamorous ancestors as one of the greatest, most luxurious and special ways of sailing the oceans, ever conceived.

SPECIFICATIONS

Country: France (built), UK (operated)

Year built: 2002–2003

Dimensions: 345m (1132ft) long; 45m (147ft 6in) wide

Weight: 151,400,000kg (167,000 tons)

Speed: 56km/h (30 knots/35mph)

Power: 117mW (157,000hp) from six engines

Passengers: 2620 plus 1253 crew

Cost: Approximately $800 million

SPECIFICATIONS

Country: USA

Year built: 1981

Dimensions:
94m (310ft) long;
21m (69ft) wide

Weight: 3,025,460kg
(3335 tons)

Service speed: 30km/h
(16 knots/18mph)

Power: 5.2mW
(7000hp) from four
engines

Passengers: 6000

Cost: $25 million

THE LARGEST FERRIES BY PASSENGER CAPACITY

STATEN ISLAND FERRY

Anything to do with New York is usually big. Think of the skyscrapers, statues and Central Park, to name but a few. To be added to that list are the Staten Island Ferries that travel between Manhattan and the borough of Staten Island. Two of them – the *Andrew J. Barberi* and the *Samuel I. Newhouse* – are the largest passenger ferries, by capacity, in the world.

The bright orange Staten Island ferries are almost as much a landmark of New York harbour as the Statue of Liberty, the icon they pass as they shuttle back and forth on their 25-minute trips between Manhattan and Staten Island. Ferries have been operating the route since the 1700s. However, a rapidly rising population and increasing mobility has resulted in the ships becoming bigger over the years.

Barberi and *Newhouse* giants

Today 19 million passengers a year are carried on the 8.4km (5.2 mile) run, 24 hours a day, 365 days a year. The total, just for one day, is almost 65,000 passengers, during 104 boat trips. Many of these are carried on the two enormous Barberi Class vessels, the giants of the fleet of nine craft. Built in 1981, the *Andrew J. Barberi* and *Samuel I. Newhouse* can carry 6000 passengers each at a service speed of 30km/h (16 knots/18mph). The former was named after a long-serving school football coach, the latter after the publisher of the *Staten Island Advance* newspaper from 1922–1979. Both of the vessels are identical in design and capabilities, and much of their capacity is a result of the fact that they are not equipped to carry vehicles, unlike other vessles in the fleet.

The service has been dubbed the biggest bargain in New York. It gives superb views and is free to travel on.

ABOVE: Two of the most familiar sights of New York Harbour – the Statue of Liberty and the square-cut, bright orange bulk of a Staten Island ferry. No cars are carried, just passengers.

THE LARGEST CRUISE SHIP (BY WIDTH)

FREEDOM OF THE SEAS

The new *Queen Mary 2* may be the largest liner around, but she was recently surpassed in size as the biggest passenger ship of them all by the *Freedom of the Seas.* With 18 decks and the sort of entertainment facilities that would more likely be found in a holiday resort than a ship, she is a prime example of how far modern technology has pushed the art of shipbuilding.

SPECIFICATIONS

Country: Turkey (Built), USA/Norway (Owned)
Year built: 2004–2006
Dimensions: 339m (1111ft 6in) long; 56m (184ft)
Total weight: 740,000,000kg (815,710 tons)
Speed: 40 km/h (21.6 knots/25 mph)
Power: 75.6mW (102,000hp)
Passengers: 3600 plus 1360 crew
Cost: $947,000,000

Imagine 37 double-decker buses parked end to end, or the Eiffel Tower laid flat on the ground (with another 16.5m/54ft added to it). Now you have some idea of just how long the *Freedom of the Seas* measures, stretching 339m (1112ft) from fore to aft.

Floating adventure

The current flagship of the Royal Caribbean Cruise Line is one of the latest leviathans to take to the oceans, and the first of three sisters – their size and cost suggesting much optimism about the future of luxury cruising. In addition to how much it cost to build, her operating costs, as of 2006, were around $1 million a day. But there's a lot to lure passengers to her. Aside from the experience of riding the biggest cruise ship afloat, she has a water park (including a wave generator), whirlpools, which extend over the ship's sides, a rock-climbing wall, all manner of shops and restaurants and even an ice-skating rink. It must almost be a disappointment having to get off when the ships calls at ports during its international trips.

BELOW: The sheer size of the *Freedom of the Seas* is such that it dwarfs all other vessels around it, as this view of the cruise ship entering port illustrates.

THE LARGEST MANNED HOT AIR BALLOON

VIRGIN PACIFIC FLYER

The Virgin Pacific Flyer balloon wasn't just the biggest manned hot-air balloon ever to fly. It set a number of records back in 1991, carrying entrepreneur Richard Branson and adventurer Per Lindstrand on the longest lighter-than-air flight in history.

There were some who dismissed Richard Branson and Per Lindstrand's balloon flight from Japan to northern Canada as little more than an over-sized publicity stunt for Branson's Virgin group of companies. They may have had a point. But as marketing ideas go, the Virgin Pacific Flyer was more epic than most, and its flight was a genuinely significant event in the history of aeronautics.

Space capsule

With a total inflatable volume of 74,000m^3 (2,600,300ft^3), the Virgin Pacific Flyer dwarfed any previous manned hot-air vessel. Built entirely to break the long-distance balloon record, as well as gain a little bit of corporate advertising on the side, it took off from Japan on January 15. It came down, albeit rather inelegantly, two days and 10,889km (6761 miles) later in northern Canada. The secret of the Flyer's success was the way it was designed to make use of the swift trans-oceanic jet streams. During the flight, it managed to reach 395km/h (245mph), an extraordinary speed for a balloon with no real form of linear propulsion, and still a record. Throughout the trip, Branson and Lindstrand survived in a pressurized pod, dubbed a 'space capsule' by some, because of the height at which the Flyer travelled.

Branson and Lindstrand teamed up again in 1998 to try to circumnavigate the world in another hot-air balloon. This attempt was less triumphant, however. They crashed in the Pacific Ocean and had to be rescued. Nothing of the size of the Virgin Pacific Flyer had ever been seen in the balloon world before.

SPECIFICATIONS	
Country: UK	
Year manufactured: 1991	
Max speed obtained: 395km/h (245 mph)	
Envelope size: 74,000m^3 (26,000,300ft^3)	
Total distance flown: 10,889km (6761 miles)	
Cost: N/A	

TOP AND LEFT: The small 'space capsule' suspended below the Virgin Pacific Flyer gave Branson and Lindstrand little room inside.

HINDENBURG/GRAF ZEPPELIN II

Prior to World War II, Germany's Zeppelin airships were the kings of the sky, and none were greater than the *Hindenburg* and the *Graf Zeppelin II*. Even 60 years after they were destroyed, they still remain the largest man-made objects ever to fly.

During the Franco-Prussian War of 1870–71, Count Ferdinand von Zeppelin became intrigued by the idea of using 'dirigible' balloons for military purposes. But even his vision could hardly have foretold the ultimate, yet tragic, realization of his dreams 60 years later.

In 1935, Zeppelin's company completed the LZ129 *Hindenburg* airship, the largest aircraft built at that time. It was subsequently equalled only by its twin-sister ship, the LZ130 *Graf Zeppelin II,* work on which started in 1936, after the *Hindenburg* went into service.

Monumental undertaking

Even in today's era of huge machines, the Zeppelins were monumental undertakings. Constructed primarily to provide scheduled flights between Germany and the United States, the *Hindenburg* was as tall as the Statue of Liberty. It was longer than three jumbo jets, but could carry just 133 people (72 passengers and 61 crew). However, this was well beyond the capacity of the biggest planes of the time, and its speed of 135km/h (84mph) meant it was able to cross the Atlantic far faster than a ship. It was simply the latest word in high-tech, luxury travel.

The *Hindenburg* was in service for just over a year before it was destroyed by fire while landing in New Jersey, USA, on 6 May 1937. The cause has never been established, but the hydrogen-filled *Hindenburg* was totally consumed in just 34 seconds, killing 36 people.

TOP AND ABOVE:
The hangars required to house the *Hindenburg* and *Graff Zeppelin II* were huge. Swastikas on the tailfins were aerial propaganda, broadcasting to the world which regime was behind these great flying machines.

SPECIFICATIONS

(FOR LZ129 *Hindenburg*)	
Country: Germany	
Year built: 1935	
Dimensions: 245m (804ft) long; by 41m (135ft) diameter	
Capacity: 133 people	
Power: 3560kW (4800hp) from four engines	
Lifting ability: 112.1 metric tons force (1.099MN)	
Cost: £500,000	

ABOVE: The *Soaring Dreams* airship makes a lively addition to an American city skyline as it flies over. The artistic exterior design is the work of 5000 children.

AMERIQUEST *SOARING DREAMS* BLIMP

It must be pretty hard to miss Ameriquest's *Soaring Dreams* passenger blimp when it flies overhead. This brightly coloured airship was decorated by almost 5000 children from 50 American cities, making it the world's largest airborne piece of art, as well as the biggest blimp around.

SPECIFICATIONS

Country: USA
Year built: 2005 (repainted)
Dimensions: 63m (206ft) long
Capacity: 10 people
Maximum speed: 93km/h (58mph)
Cost: N/A

The 'official' term for this kind of craft is 'non-rigid', as it doesn't have an internal framework like other airships. Prior to 2005, Ameriquest's airship *Liberty* was used purely for advertising the US lending company, so it was patriotically finished in the Stars and Stripes livery, along with the firm's logo. An idea called the Soaring Dreams Project saw American children paint different parts of a 12,192m (40,000ft) canvas during that year, which was then fixed to the airship. A colossal 1703.5 litres (450 gallons) of paint were used, and the covering added 635kg (1400lb) to the blimp's overall weight. The result is probably the most flamboyant aircraft ever to fly.

With a capacity of 10 people, including the pilot and co-pilot, the *Soaring Dreams* passenger blimp has become a familiar sight, turning up at major outdoor events. Its length when fully inflated is 69m (206ft), and the craft has a cruising speed of 72km/h (45mph), meaning that it can take up to three weeks for it to cross America from coast to coast. One of its more unusual features is that it has the ability to hover, making it one of only two airships in the US with this feature.

THE LARGEST BIPLANE, STILL FLYING

REPLICA VICKERS VIMY

The original Vickers Vimy was a heavy British bomber aircraft. It entered service right at the end of World War I, and when peace arrived, it became a long-distance commercial plane instead. A modern replica built in the 1990s is now the largest biplane still in operation.

SPECIFICATIONS

Country: Australia/USA
Year built: 1992–1994 (based on 1917 design)
Dimensions: 13.3m (43ft 6in) long; 21m (68ft) wingspan
Capacity: 2 people
Maximum speed: 165km/h (100mph)
Power: 1200hp (894kW) from two engines
Cost: N/A

LEFT AND ABOVE: Replica Vickers Vimy biplane is a tribute to one of the greatest of early twentieth century aircraft.

Why build a 'new' version of a plane that went out of production almost 80 years ago? Well, the ponderous but powerful Vickers Vimy epitomized cutting-edge technology back at the end of World War I, and achieved a number of firsts. In 1919, for example, a Vickers Vimy became the first airplane to cross the Atlantic nonstop, and this was soon followed by a flight from London to Darwin in Australia. And in 1922, one set off from London to fly to South Africa, although it crashed en route.

Something old, something new

An Australian/American team therefore decided to construct a replica to re-enact these three pioneering flights. Taking 17 months to build, the result was a biplane that stayed as true as possible to the original blueprints, albeit with some modern concessions. For example, the two Rolls-Royce engines used originally gave way to Chevrolet V8 car engines, and instead of a wooden frame, the new Vickers has steel tubing.

The 1990s version proved just as capable of coping with long distances as the real thing. In 1994, the flight from England to Australia was achieved. The year 2000 saw London to South Africa conquered, which is more than a real Vimy managed. In 2005, the re-born Vickers crossed the Atlantic. It continues to fly at displays as a working monument to one of the great aircraft from the early days of flight.

CAPRONI CA-60 TRANSAERO

The history of aviation is littered with fantastic one-offs that promised much, but ultimately delivered little. One of the most extraordinary was Caproni's Ca-60 seaplane. This amazing creation was the product of a theory that the more wings a plane had, the better it would fly. This turned out not to be the case, however.

BELOW: The Transaero was an extraordinary-looking contraption, and it wasn't a surprise that this imaginative design was inherently un-airworthy. Its test flight ended in total disaster in the middle of a lake.

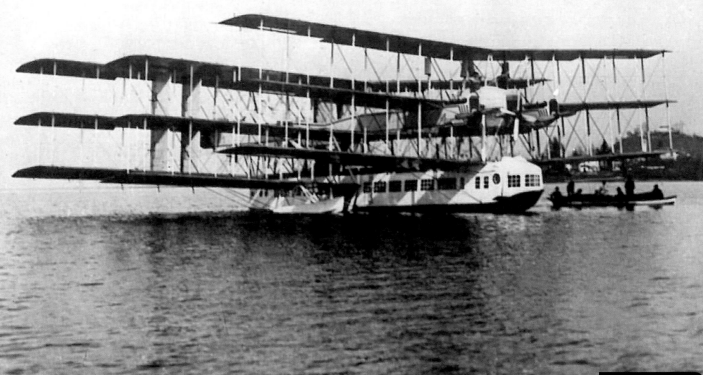

The idea behind the Caproni Ca-60 was that it would provide a transatlantic passenger service for between 100 and 150 passengers – something that, at the time, no other aircraft could offer. The thinking was sound enough, but the aircraft that subsequently materialized was little short of mad, although remarkable to look at. Its designers reasoned that the more wings and engines it was fitted with, the better able it would be to fly long distances.

Slowly up, quickly down

Or not, as things turned out. In 1920, one experimental model was built. It had three banks of three wings (left over

from bombers that took part in World War I) and eight engines. Its first test flight was in March 1921 from Lake Maggiore, in Italy. The ungainly machine managed to struggle to a height of 18m (60ft) before it simply collapsed and took a nosedive into the lake, killing both pilots. Although it was obvious to most people that the whole thing was simply too ambitious to fly, an attempt was made to repair it. Then a mysterious fire completely destroyed it for good.

Despite its failure, the Triple Hydro-tri-plane, as the Ca-60 was dubbed, was fascinating. No one before, or since, has attempted to build an airplane with so many wings.

SPECIFICATIONS

Country: Italy
Year built: 1920
Dimensions:
23m (77ft) long;
30m (98ft 6in) wingspan
Capacity: 100 passengers
Weight (loaded):
26,000kg (29 tons)
Cruising speed:
130km/h (80mph)
Power: 2400kW (3200hp) from eight engines
Cost: N/A

SPECIFICATIONS

Country: USA
Year built: 1942–1947
Dimensions:
67m (219ft) long;
97.5m (320ft) wingspan
Weight (loaded):
180,000kg (198 tons)
Cruising speed:
320km/h (220mph)
Power: 17,897kW
(24,000hp) from eight
engines
Cost: $23 million

THE LARGEST WOODEN AIRCRAFT/THE LARGEST WINGSPAN EVER

HUGHES H-4
SPRUCE GOOSE

Contrary to popular belief, Howard Hughes' gigantic H4 Hercules flying boat wasn't the largest aircraft of all time. However, it does still hold the record for having been the biggest wooden airplane and flying boat, as well as having the largest ever wingspan.

TOP, ABOVE RIGHT AND BACKGROUND: It travelled on water, it travelled on the ground...but flying proved more tricky for the *Spruce Goose.*

In the annals of aviation, no plane has ever inspired so much controversy and notoriety as the *Spruce Goose* – a derogatory nickname that Howard Hughes, the man behind it, hated. But cut through all the intrigue and scandal surrounding the *Spruce Goose,* and you are left with one of the world's most astonishing flying machines ever.

Herculean task

The inspiration behind the H-4 Hercules was to provide wartime transport for troops and cargo across the Atlantic. From the start, the intention had always been to build it from wood to save metal for the military effort. However, by the time the huge craft was complete, World War II had been over for two years, and Hughes was called to account for the massive amount of money that had been spent. To prove a point, during engine tests, he decided to try and get the H-4 airborne. In November 1947, the *Spruce Goose* managed to fly 1.6km (1 mile) at an altitude of 20m (70ft), attaining a speed of 130km/h (80mph) before landing again on the waters of Long Beach, California. However, the H-4 never flew again. It was maintained in flying condition until Hughes died in 1976, after which the *Spruce Goose* became a museum piece. It still remains on display today, a monument both to engineering folly and audacious far-sightedness.

THE LARGEST BOMBER, CURRENT

BOEING B-52 STRATOFORTRESS

It seems a little chilling referring to an immensely destructive aircraft as 'successful', but the B-52 Stratofortress deserves the accolade for its longevity as well as abilities. It has been in service with the US Air Force since 1954, and still plays a frontline role as the largest bomber in existence.

SPECIFICATIONS

Country: USA
Year built: 1952–1962
Dimensions:
48.5m (159ft 6in) long;
56.5m (185ft) wingspan
Weight: (loaded)
120,000kg (132 tons)
Maximum speed:
1000km/h (650mph)
Power: 608kN
(136,000lbf) from eight
jet engines
Cost: $9.28 million
(1962)

The career of the B-52 Stratofortress has been little short of extraordinary. It was introduced in 1955, yet still flies (and fights) today, and the plan is that it will remain on duty until around 2050. That a century-old design will still be regarded as a valid military force speaks volumes about how inherently good the B-52 is at its job. And with the last example built in 1962, those planes still in action in the middle of the twenty-first century will be around 90 years old.

Big and Buff

Nicknamed the 'Buff', the B-52's original raison d'être was to fly long-distance nuclear missions to Russia, if required. Squadrons were kept at a constant state of readiness, able to take off within a few minutes' notice. But the B-52 has since proved itself capable of functioning just as easily as a conventional bomber at any altitude. However, of the 744 models built, only 85 remain on the Air Force's books. These have been constantly updated with the latest technology.

The most recognizable feature of the B-52 – apart from its substantial dimensions – is its set of eight turbojet engines slung out in groups of two below the wings. Each one is capable of developing a thrust of 76kN (17,000lbf).

ABOVE AND BELOW: Eight jet engines power the enormous B-52. This deadly but chilling shape should still be in the skies over 40 years from now.

THE LARGEST SUPERSONIC AIRCRAFT

CONCORDE

Rarely does mankind take a technological step backwards, but when Concorde stopped flying in 2003, the era of supersonic commercial jet travel came to an end. More than just a very fast airline, Concorde was one of the most striking machines ever created. She was an icon to all those who travelled on her, and the many more who longed to.

TOP AND ABOVE: From any angle, Concorde was – and is – an extraordinarily handsome aircraft, and its looks never seem to age.

Like many of the world's most inspirational machines, Concorde wasn't actually a success. Conceived in the optimistic 1960s, the graceful delta-winged aircraft was intended to introduce the masses to air travel at faster than the speed of sound. However, by the time the aircraft went into service in 1973 orders had fallen through, development costs were 600 per cent over estimate, and pollution and noise worries meant that the aircraft was banned from many of the world's airports. Thus, only 20 (including prototypes) were built. British Airways and Air France put them in to service.

Elegance

However, few white elephants have been so beautiful as Concorde. Despite being conceived over 40 years ago, the design still looks futuristic and elegant. And it did, eventually, become a success, establishing itself as the ultimate, if expensive, way to fly the Atlantic. Concorde embodied luxury, power and speed blended together in an engineering aviation miracle, capable of moving at a mile every 2.7 seconds. When it was finally withdrawn from service, millions, particularly in France and the UK, watched the final flights on TV. It remains one of the most famous airplanes in the world. Its profile, with 'droop nose' used for take-off and landing, has made it the most recognizable.

BOEING 747

No book on mega machines could be truly complete without mentioning the Boeing 747. It has recently been superseded as the biggest airliner, but for over 35 years there was simply nothing bigger an ordinary passenger could fly on. The Boeing 747 revolutionized air travel for the masses.

BELOW: The Jumbo shape is familiar to millions, and a common sight at major airports.

When the 747 was jointly conceived by Pan Am and Boeing in 1965, it was like nothing that had been dreamt up before. They envisioned a giant jet aircraft capable of carrying up to 524 passengers in spacious comfort. The project could have been a financial disaster, but from the moment the 747, nicknamed the jumbo jet, entered service in 1970 it was a resounding success, and has since become the mainstay of long-distance, popular air routes. When a lot of people want to go a long way, it's invariably a Jumbo Jet that will take them there.

The Jumbo's hump

Operated by practically every major airline across the world, over 1430 Jumbos have been built.

Production of the 747-400 continues to this day, demonstrating just how inherently 'right' the original design was. Only the Hughes H-4 Spruce Goose could boast a wingspan that was greater than that of a 747. But one of the 747's other radical features, which soon became the Jumbo's most recognizable trademark, was the second short deck above the main deck. The 'hump' was added in case the 747 failed to become successful as a passenger aircraft. By moving the cockpit, and some of the passenger accommodation, to a higher level, a loading door in the nose could be incorporated so the Jumbo could easily be converted into a cargo transporter.

SPECIFICATIONS

Country: USA

Year built from: 1969

Dimensions: 70.5m (232ft) long; 64.5m (211ft 6in) wingspan

Capacity: Up to 524 passengers, depending on configuration

Weight: 362,880kg (400 tons)

Maximum speed: Mach 0.92/1127km/h (700mph)

Power: 1096kN (245,997lbf) from four engines

Cost: $275 million (2005)

THE LARGEST COMMERCIAL JET, IMPENDING

AIRBUS A380

Once it was the Jumbo that was the king of the commercial passenger skies. Now the crown has been taken by the Superjumbo, the nickname the Airbus A380 has already been christened with, despite the fact that it has only just entered service.

SPECIFICATIONS

Country: Europe

Year built from: 2002

Dimensions: 73m (239ft 6in) long; 80m (261ft) wingspan

Capacity: Up to 853 passengers, depending on configuration

Weight (empty): 276,800kg (305 tons)

Maximum speed: 0.89 Mach/977.04km/h (602.6mph)

Power: 1360kN (306,000lbf) from four engines

Cost: $296–316 million (as of 2006)

Even a substantial Boeing 747 looks humble sitting next to a new Airbus A380. This is the world's only double-decker airliner, and it has over 50 per cent more floor space than a 747. It is capable of seating a maximum of 853 people, which is over 300 more than a Jumbo can manage at full stretch.

Boeing breaker

The A380 was developed to break Boeing's dominance of the high-capacity aircraft market. Expanding significantly larger in terms of length wasn't a viable option. Instead, the A380 went taller, with an extra full-length deck added along its top. Building started in 2002, with various components constructed throughout Europe. The first prototype was unveiled in 2005, with deliveries in 2006.

The A380 surpasses the 747 in practically every way. It is longer, taller and has a bigger wingspan, although this still falls 7.5m (24ft 6in) short of the wingspan of Hughes' H-4 Spruce Goose of 60 years earlier. Despite having extra power, it's more economical, and the 'fly-by-wire' technology (whereby it uses electronic systems rather than hydraulic and mechanical parts) makes it easier to pilot and more manoeuvrable. However, it's not quite as fast as a 747, but the difference adds up to only about 100km/h (62mph).

LEFT AND ABOVE: Up to 853 people can be carried by the new Airbus A380.

THE LARGEST SOLAR POWERED AIRCRAFT
NASA HELIOS

With ever-increasing concern about the future of the environment, some alternative to fossil fuels needs to be found. So, what impact will this have on the future of air transport? Until it met with disaster, one of the goals behind NASA's Helios project was to explore this very question.

ABOVE AND BELOW: The flexible design of the solar powered Helios allowed it to bend while in flight.

SPECIFICATIONS

Country: USA	
Year manufactured: 1999	
Dimensions: 3.6m (12ft) long; 75m (247ft) wingspan	
Maximum speed: 273.5km/h (170mph)	
Weight: (loaded): 929kg (2048lb)	
Power: 21kW (28hp) from 14 propeller engines	
Cost: $1 million	

Radical in concept and looks, NASA's Helios electrically powered aircraft could have offered an alternative to environmentally damaging air travel. It was a unique aircraft, taking its power from the sun by day, and from regenerative fuel cells at night, making possible flights lasting for weeks or even months without the need to land. And this would be accomplished without pollution, because no consumable fuel was used.

Ocean failure

Although unmanned and controlled by remote, Helios was able to carry a 272kg (600lb) payload – the equivalent of over 40 average humans – up to 21km (70,000ft). During one flight, it reached 29.5km (96,863ft), where the atmosphere is similar to that of Mars. This enabled scientists to collect useful data for potential missions to this planet. There was also an intention to fly the craft, uninterrupted, for 96 hours during another test. Unfortunately, Helios never had the opportunity to attempt this. In June 2003, while flying over the Pacific near Hawaii, it broke up and fell into the sea, and all of its experimental technology was completely lost.

However, so promising were the results from Helios that NASA intends to continue its research into so-called 'atmospheric satellites'. It is likely then, that before too long, the offspring of Helios will once again soar to high altitudes in the name of environmental and space research.

THE LARGEST 'STEALTH' RECONNAISSANCE AIRCRAFT

LOCKHEED SR-71 BLACKBIRD

It's somewhat ironic that one of the first 'stealth' aircraft – the SR-71 Blackbird – should eventually become one of the world's most famous military planes, thanks to its futuristic design and astounding performance.

The world's largest stealth reconnaissance aircraft sounds rather like a contradiction in terms. After all, if you want something not to be noticed, surely it's best to make it as small as possible? In fact, by general military aircraft standards, the SR-71 Blackbird is a compact aircraft, especially considering its flight capabilities. And its shape was designed to make it more difficult for radar to pick up – although in truth, as radar technology progressed, the Blackbird soon became highly noticeable on hostile screens. However, so high and so fast did the SR-71 fly that no missile could ever catch it.

Ironing out the wrinkles

The SR-71 first took to the skies in 1966, and was an extraordinary-looking machine for the time. Indeed, it remains so to this day, despite the fact that the last one was retired in 1998. Able to fly at three times the speed of sound, and at altitudes of up to 30,000m (100,000ft), the Blackbird was painted in a menacing matt radar-absorbent black paint and skinned in titanium alloy. The latter is very resistant to the heat encountered at high altitudes, though it was still common for the aircraft's nose to be wrinkled after landing. Ground crews would have to smooth it out again using a blowtorch!

The SR-71 still holds the record for the quickest flight between New York and London, achieving the feat in just 1 hour, 55 minutes. By comparison, a Jumbo jet takes around six hours, and Concorde could do the same distance in around 3 hours, 20 minutes.

ABOVE: From any angle, but especially above, the SR-71 looked utterly intimidating. Sleek lines and two enormous jet engines were the secret to its ability to fly higher and faster than anything else in its day.

SPECIFICATIONS

Country: USA
Years built: 1964–1969
Dimensions: 33m (107ft 6in) long; 17m (55ft 6in) wingspan
Weight: (loaded): 77,000kg (85 tons)
Maximum speed: Mach 3.3 plus /3530km/h (2190mph)
Power: 290kN (65,000lbf) from two engines
Cost: $34 million

THE LARGEST TANDEM ROTOR HELICOPTER, CURRENT

BOEING CH-47 CHINOOK

Helicopters aren't best known for their lifting abilities. They're usually lightweight machines in which the emphasis is on speed and manoeuvrability rather than carrying heavy weights. However, the CH-47 Chinook, currently the world's biggest tandem-rotor helicopter, is capable of transporting quite significant loads.

SPECIFICATIONS

Country: USA

Year built from: 1961

Dimensions: 30m (90ft) long; 18m (60ft) rotor diameter

Weight (loaded): 12,100kg (13 tons)

Maximum speed: 315km/h (196mph)

Power: 5600kW (10,138hp) from two engines

Cost: Approximately $32 million (1995)

LEFT: Long-bladed tandem rotors and two powerful engines give the CH-47 Chinook the ability to transport tanks and aircraft, making it a useful tool during battle conditions.

What makes the CH-47 Chinook so adept at heavy transport? Unlike conventional helicopters, both of its rotors are horizontally mounted, and rotate in opposite directions to each other. That eliminates the need for a vertical motor at the rear (as most other helicopters have), to counteract the twist effects of the main rotor. This means all its power can be used for lift and thrust. Under battlefield conditions, the CH-47 can carry up to 33 troops and/or items of artillery more quickly than a land vehicle could manage and with more versatility than a fixed-wing aircraft. Its under-slung payload maximum is up to 11,793kg (13 tons), meaning it can even manage bulldozers and loaded shipping containers.

Military and civilian

This is one of the most successful helicopter designs ever, and over 1000 Chinooks have been built and sold to 16 countries. Their use isn't just military, either. The civilian version is commonly used for construction and logging, and, with a water dispenser slung below it, for fighting fires.

First flown in 1961, the Chinook has proved its value in most major US conflicts since Vietnam, where one of its major roles was the recovery of downed aircraft. Indeed, Chinooks managed to retrieve over 12,000 planes. The CH-47 may be approaching its fiftieth birthday, but to users like the US Army and the Royal Air Force, and others around the world, it's still a vital piece of military equipment.

Nothing like the Mil Mi-12 had been constructed before production of the first prototype was begun in 1965. And since the cancellation of the project in the early 1970s, no company has attempted to build anything else quite so huge and complicated.

The Mi-12's design brief was that it had to be capable of lifting up to 30,000kg (33 tons), more than any other helicopter had ever managed. In fact, thanks to its ingenious but somewhat eccentric design, the 'Homer' (as NATO dubbed the craft) proved itself more than capable of this feat, hauling a payload of 44,205kg (49 tons) up to a height of 2255m (7400ft) – a record that still stands today.

Four rotors and engines

The Mi-12 gained such a superb ability from its four rotors, with contra-rotating pairs mounted facing upwards on each wing, in an arrangement known as a two-rotor transverse system. Four gas-turbine engines, which were also mounted on the wings, powered the rotors. Yet despite the Mi-12 proving its worth, only two models were built before it was decided to end production. Rumour has it that a third experimental helicopter was constructed, but crashed during testing. If this is true, it may have been the reason for the end of the scheme. The original two Mi-12s are now museum pieces, and are unlikely to ever fly again.

BELOW AND ABOVE: The Mi-12's innovative design – two contra-rotating rotors to each wing – allowed it to lift more than any other helicopter.

THE LARGEST HELICOPTER, EVER

MIL MI-12 'HOMER'

Looking like a cross between a fixed-wing aircraft and a tandem-rotor helicopter, the Mil Mi-24 may have been one of the world's more bizarre aircraft designs, but its lifting capabilities were very impressive. And it still holds the record as the biggest helicopter ever built.

THE LARGEST BALLISTIC MISSILE
R-36 ICBM

During the Cold War, a continual game of oneupmanship was played out between the Soviet Union and the United States and Western Europe. If one side built something big, then the other side had to have its equivalent as well, only just a little larger. However, it was the USSR that eventually ended up with the largest missile in the world. Its nuclear R-36 was such a threatening weapon that it was dubbed the 'City Buster'.

Conceived during the peak of the Cold War in April 1962, the R-36 family were massive missiles that could also be used as space launchers. They were of such size and destructive force that they were regarded as one of the USSR's most serious threats. Thus, when the Soviet Union broke up in 1991, the R-36s were one of the targets the US sought to reduce by arms treaty.

Catastrophic consequences

The two-stage R-36s could carry a range of potent nuclear weaponry from a five-megaton nuclear device up to a highly destructive 20-megaton warhead. Of even more concern to the West were the versions that could carry up to 10 smaller warheads and, at one point, an upgrade was considered that would have allowed the R-36 to yield 38 nuclear devices. Just one of these versions could have had catastrophic consequences if launched in a strike.

In 1991, it was discovered that 308 R-36 silos were operational – ready to fire at short notice. Around 85 remain, and although by 2009 the number should go down to 40, these will continue serving until 2014 at least. The R-36 menace has not yet gone away though the Cold War has.

ABOVE AND BELOW: The traditional Soviet May Day Parade was one of the few times the public got to see an R-36 ICBM.

SPECIFICATIONS

Country: Russia (USSR)

Years built:
1965–1991

Dimensions:
32m (105ft 6in) long;
3m (10ft) diameter

Weight: 183,000kg
(201 tons)

Maximum speed:
8km/sec (5 miles/sec)

Lift-off thrust: 2366kW
(531,965lbf)

Cost: 8–10 billion
Roubles (research,
development and
testing)

THE LARGEST FLYING 'OFFICE'

AIR FORCE ONE

ABOVE: Air Force One always comes to a standstill with its left side facing onlookers, to protect the President's quarters, on the right side, from potential attack.

The American Presidential Boeing 747-200B can justifiably be called the largest flying office in the world, or perhaps even the largest flying government building in the world. It has all the facilities needed to continue the running of the United States while the President is on board.

SPECIFICATIONS

Country: USA
Year built: 1990
Dimensions:
71m (232ft) long; 60m (195ft 6in) wingspan
Weight: (Estimated, loaded) 375,000kg (413 tons)
Maximum speed: Mach 0.92/1014km/h (630mph)
Power: 1000kN (226,800lbf) from four engines
Cost: N/A

Air Force One has been the call sign used for any USAF aircraft carrying the President of the United States since 1953. However, the term is generally recognized by the public as being the designation of the Boeing 747-200B in the distinctive 'United States of America' design. There are actually two, identical, 747s, which were introduced in 1990. Both take off almost simultaneously to foil any possible terrorist attack, by creating confusion as to which one the President is actually aboard.

Flying White House

Heavily modified from a standard Boeing 747, Air Force One's features and furnishings include enough storage for 2000 meals, two galleys that can cater for up to 100 people at a time, medical facilities (a doctor is always on board), guest and staff sleeping quarters, and extensive offices, with 85 telephones and 19 televisions, plus all other essential communications equipment. The President himself has a suite and a private dressing room, workout room, lavatory, shower and private office. Effectively, Air Force One is almost the White House with wings.

In the event of a national crisis or threat, Air Force One can keep flying indefinitely, thanks to its aerial refuelling capability. It is also fitted with anti-attack systems – many of which are classified – although at all times, the plane flies with fighter escorts as well.

THE LARGEST SPACE ROCKET

SATURN V

The largest, most powerful and most successful space rocket of all time remains the Saturn V launcher. It was responsible for taking man to the Moon and for putting the first US space station in orbit.

I n 1961, President John F Kennedy announced that the United States would try to land a man on the Moon before the end of the 1960s. One major barrier to this goal was that there were no rockets powerful enough at the time to carry a person all the way to the lunar surface.

Under Wernher von Braun, the director of NASA, scientists at the Marshall Space Flight Center in Huntsville, Alabama, gradually developed a series of Saturn launchers to achieve Kennedy's dream. The culmination was the enormous Saturn V. This three-stage rocket was huge compared not just to other existing launchers, but also to other manmade structures. For example, at 111m (364ft) tall, it measured only 30cm (12in) shorter than St Paul's Cathedral in London.

First flight

The first Saturn V launch was in 1967, carrying the unmanned Apollo 4 spacecraft. A year later, the first Saturn V manned mission was undertaken, with Apollo 8.

But the rocket's greatest moment came on 16 July 1969, when it blasted off for the Moon with the Apollo 11 capsule. The mission to land was a success, and the Saturn V, as well as the crew of Apollo 11, became the stuff of space legend.

Further landings followed, until the cancellation of the Apollo programme, after which Saturn V was used to help launch the Skylab space station in 1973. It was to be the culmination of the monster rocket's career, during which no payload was ever lost. With thoughts turning to cheaper and easier ways to fly to the stars, the Saturn V fell away in favour of what was to become the Space Shuttle. Three examples remain on display, however, as a testament to the most powerful of engines ever created.

RIGHT: The roar from the first launch of Saturn V could be heard miles away.

SPECIFICATIONS

Country: USA
Year manufactured from: 1967
Dimensions: 58m (190ft) in length; 11.5m (38ft) in diameter
Payload: 118,000kg (130 tons)
Lift-off thrust: 12,494kN (1400 tons)
Cost: $200 million

LEFT: And this is what it was all about – the command module once atop the Saturn V, after all the rocket stages had been shed.

RIGHT: The Russian Space Shuttle, which used the Energia to launch it. The Buran shuttle flew only once, and Energia only twice.

THE LARGEST RUSSIAN SPACE ROCKET

ENERGIA

When the USA announced its plans for a reusable spacecraft – the Space Shuttle – it was predictable that the Soviet Union would start working towards the same goal. At that time, the USA and the USSR were locked in the space race – a competition to outdo each other in space.

I n the end, the Buran Shuttle, which was the name of the Russian attempt to build a version of the US Space Shuttle, was aborted. The launch system for the failed Buran was a rocket called the Energia. It flew only twice, yet its size and power made it significant because it was the only rocket ever to come close to the United States' mighty Saturn V.

Development on the Energia, which was also intended to serve as an expendable heavy-duty booster for conventional flights, started in 1976. The plan was to have three different variants for different payloads: the larger the weight being carried, the more supplementary booster rockets could be attached to the main body. The ultimate Energia – which never actually flew – would have had eight strap-on boosters. This would have given it enough power to carry 175,200kg (192 tons) into space, a much greater

amount than the 120,000kg (132 tons) the Saturn V model could carry. Fittingly, the name for this version of the Energia was Hercules (though it was christened Vulcan as well).

Doomed by politics

But political, not technical, issues spelt doom for the Energia. The first one flew in 1987, carrying a military satellite. A year later, the Buran Shuttle successfully lifted off on the back of an Energia. Then came the fall of the Soviet Union. The Energia and Buran Shuttle programmes were cancelled, and the equipment was put in to mothballs.

Parts of the Energia system live on in current rockets. But in the same way that the United States now has nothing to compare to its old Saturn V, so current Russian launch systems are mere shadows of the mighty Energia.

SPECIFICATIONS

Country: Russia (USSR)
Year manufactured: 1987
Dimensions: 97m (318ft) long; 7.75m (25ft) in diameter
Payload: Up to 175,200kg (192 tons)
Lift-off thrust: 35,129.900kN (7,897,516lbf)
Cost: $764 million

SPECIFICATIONS

Country: USA
Year built: 1961–1972
Dimensions: CM: 3.47m (11ft) long by 3.90m (13ft) in diameter; SM: 7.56m (25ft) long by 3.90m (13ft) in diameter; LM: 3.54m (11ft 6in) long by 4.27m (14ft) in diameter
Service module engine thrust: 600kN (11 tons)
Payload: N/A
Cost: Approximately $24 billion, total Apollo series

LEFT: An Apollo space capsule is recovered from the ocean. The damage to the outer surface is caused by the heat of re-entry.

THE LARGEST MANNED SPACE CAPSULE

APOLLO MANNED SPACE CAPSULE

Prior to the Space Shuttle, manned capsules had to be quite small so that early rockets could lift them in to space. Being small also made it easier for a space capsule to parachute back to Earth safely. But the Apollo crafts were bigger than most.

The US Apollo Program was the name given to the project designed to land astronauts on the Moon. The launch system they used consisted of manned capsules mounted at the top of huge rockets, such as the Saturn V. With previous manned space flights, all the crew really had to do was orbit the Earth, and then land successfully. For Apollo, though, there was an extra, rather important aspect. The goal was to launch a vehicle to the Moon and return it to Earth safely.

Larger than earlier craft

This meant that the Apollo capsules were much larger than earlier craft. They consisted of three different sections: the Command Module (CM) at the top; the Service Module (SM) in the middle; and the Lunar Module (LM) at the bottom. The Command Module was, as its name suggests,

the control centre of the spacecraft, as well as the crew's main living quarters. Mounted on to this was the service module, which contained essential equipment vital to the mission, such as fuel cells, batteries, water and oxygen, plus the rocket engine that was used to get Apollo in and out of lunar orbit. And underneath this was the Lunar Module: the moon-landing vehicle itself. All this was enclosed by what was known as an SLA, which stands for the Spacecraft Lunar Module Adapter. The SLA was simply four long aluminium panels that made the whole capsule streamlined when taking off. Once the capsule was safely launched into space, the SLA was detonated away.

By the time the Apollo spacecraft returned to Earth, it was considerably smaller, having shed its other attachments. The reduced size enabled the capsule to float down into the ocean.

THE LARGEST PLANETARY VEHICLE
LUNAR ROVER

On Earth, a Lunar Rover wouldn't be a mega machine at all. In reality, it is little bigger than a very basic beach buggy with a few high-tech gizmos attached. On the Moon, however, such a vehicle allowed astronauts far greater freedom than before.

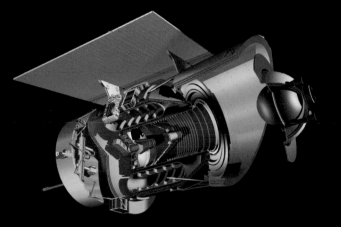

ABOVE AND BELOW: The Lunar Rovers gave astronauts far greater freedom on the Moon than they had before. And they're all still up there.

Only four Lunar Rovers were ever built in total (one each for Apollo 15, 16 and 17 plus another for spare parts after the Apollo programme was cancelled), but their importance to the exploration of the Moon was significant. No longer were astronauts confined to staying around the Lunar Module, and instead could travel some distance away from the landing zone. On the Apollo 17, the final mission to the Moon, the Lunar Rover travelled 7.6km (almost 5 miles) away from the Lunar Module. That may not sound like much, but it was by far the longest distance any machine has been driven on the surface of Earth's natural satellite.

A sports car on the moon

With a top speed of about 13km/h (8mph) and only 744kW (1hp) total power (thanks to the lack of gravity, this was all that was needed), the Lunar Rovers were far from fast. However, they did have a chassis similar to that of a sports car, made up of aluminium alloy tubing and featuring double wishbone suspension. This made them manoeuvrable and rugged. But they were also lightweight, an essential factor allowing them to be carried in the Apollo Lunar Module. One thing that did distinguish the Rovers from conventional Earth vehicles was the large antenna dish mounted on the front of the vehicle. Other bits of equipment included film and TV cameras, and a toolkit, just in case.

Despite their light weight, the Lunar Rovers could not be brought back to Earth from the Moon, so that's where the three of them remain to this day, joined by two of the Soviet Union's two unmanned Rovers Lunokhod 1 and Lunokhod 2. With no definite plans for people to land on the Moon in the foreseeable future, they're all likely to be parked there for quite some time to come.

SPECIFICATIONS

Country: USA
Year built: 1971
Dimensions: 3.1m (10ft) long; 1.14m (4ft) high
Payload: 490kg (1,080lb)
Power: 744kW (1hp) from four 186kW (0.25hp) motors on each wheel
Cost: Approximately $38 million

LEFT: This illustration is of Hubble, way out beyond the Earth's atmosphere.

THE LARGEST SPACE TELESCOPE

HUBBLE SPACE TELESCOPE

The best images of space are taken without the interference of Earth's atmosphere. And that's exactly what the Hubble Space Telescope (HST), in orbit around our planet, is able to provide. It's not just the largest telescope in space, but one of the most significant telescopes ever built.

The idea of Hubble (named after a leading American Astronomer Edwin Powell Hubble) was first mooted in 1946, well before humanity had ever launched anything into space. But it took until 1990, after a difficult and protracted development, for Hubble to be sent in to space. Unfortunately, the difficulties didn't end once it was up there. Problems were found with its main mirror, meaning the HST's abilities to view were seriously compromised. Thanks to the Space Shuttle, repairs were successfully undertaken, and Hubble reached its full potential in 1993. Since then, it has become an incredibly useful astronomical tool.

Hubble contains five scientific instruments of varying types, including cameras, spectrographs and photometers. It's made some spectacular discoveries and recorded amazing images, including the formation of new stars, supernovae and a comet collision with Jupiter (something that only happens once every few centuries). The HST has even helped scientists work out how old the universe actually is.

Despite its usefulness, Hubble's life span is limited, and it is due to be replaced by an even larger item – the James Webb Space Telescope – in 2013. By that time, however, Hubble might not be around to witness the change. Unless adjustments are made to Hubble's gyroscopes, its current orbit will result in it burning up in Earth's atmosphere sometime from 2010 onwards. As yet, no definite decision has been made as to whether or not these adjustments will be made.

NASA'S CHANDRA X-RAY TELESCOPE

The Earth's atmosphere absorbs most X-rays from space. This meant that an orbiting telescope was needed to observe this space phenomenon, so NASA launched the Chandra space telescope – the heaviest item ever to be launched – in 1999.

Named after the Indian-American physicist Subrahmanyan Chandrasekhar, the Chandra Telescope is one of NASA's four 'Great Observatories' in orbit around Earth. Its purpose lies in the field of X-ray astronomy, something that can't easily be carried out from the planet itself because of atmospheric interference.

RIGHT AND BELOW: The Chandra X-ray telescope, filling practically the entire loading bay of the Space Shuttle Columbia shortly before its launch. When in orbit, its solar panels unfolded to provide power, as shown left.

Heavy load

First proposed in 1976, work started on the instrument the following year. Progress was slow, and it was only in the 1990s, after the telescope was redesigned to cut costs, that its construction accelerated. When the Space Shuttle *Columbia* took it into space in 1999, it was the heaviest item ever to be carried by the craft, the extra weight being the booster rocket system needed to take it into an orbit beyond the reach of the shuttle.

It currently circumnavigates the globe at a distance approximately one-third of the way towards the Moon. This means that, should Chandra ever go wrong, it won't be possible to repair it, but it also puts it above the planet's radiation belt, ensuring that its delicate instruments are out of harm's way. Despite this, its imaging spectrometer has already suffered minor damage from radiation particles. Luckily, this hasn't compromised the telescope's effectiveness or the data it has transmitted back to its base at the Chandra X-ray Center in Cambridge, Massachusetts.

SPECIFICATIONS

Country: USA
Year built: 1976–1999
Dimensions: 17.5m (57ft) long
Weight: 24,000kg (26.5 tons)
Orbit height: 87,000 miles (140,000km)
Cost: $1.5 billion; $2.8 billion to operate

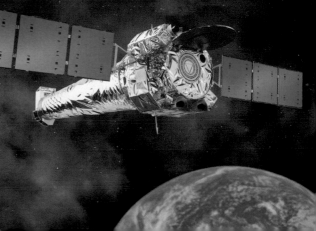

THE BIGGEST SPACE STATION

INTERNATIONAL SPACE STATION

The International Space Station truly lives up to its name as a co-operative effort between many countries to maintain a continuous human presence in space. Although fully functioning at the moment, it is still being built. This means the largest man-made object in space will gradually get bigger still.

Space stations are usually the stuff of science fiction. But they've also been science fact since 1971, when Russia launched its Salyut 1 station. The International Space Station is currently the only manned station in orbit around the Earth, and therefore the largest human space machine. This US-conceived project is a genuine global effort with involvement from Russia, Japan, Canada and Brazil, plus the countries of the European Space Agency.

Space jigsaw

Because of its modular construction, different components can gradually be added on to the ISS. The first piece of the jigsaw – a cargo module – was launched in 1998, two other sections having to be added before the first crew could join. This happened in 2000.

The ISS was due to be completed by 2005, but the grounding of Space Shuttle upset this schedule. It is now conceived that the station will be complete by 2010, by which time it will hold a crew of six (current capacity is three). Extra laboratories will allow the ISS to expand its research potential as well. The most noticeable features of the station are its huge solar panels, which provide all the power for its various functions, including life support.

Famous just for being itself, the ISS also made the headlines when it became the venue for the first space wedding. A cosmonaut on the station, Yuri Malenchenko, married Ekaterina Dmitriev in 2003. His bride, though, was in Texas at the time. The ISS has also been the 'holiday' location for three space tourists.

SPECIFICATIONS

Country: Multinational
Year built: 1998–2010 (projected)
Distance from Earth (Current): 42 million km (26 million miles)
Dimensions: (Current): 44.5m (146ft) long; 73m (239ft 6in) wide
Weight (Current): 183,300kg (202 tons)
Cost: $100 billion (projected)

LEFT: The modular construction of the International Space Station can clearly be seen in this illustration from above. There's still more to be added.

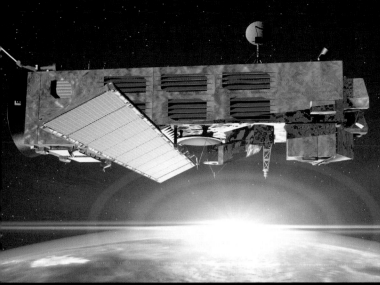

ABOVE: An illustration of ENVISAT in space with its solar panels unfolded.
RIGHT: ENVISAT pictured during its painstaking construction on Earth, mounted on a moveable platform.

THE LARGEST EARTH OBSERVATION SATELLITE

ENVISAT
(ENVIRONMENTAL SATELLITE)

One of the best places to observe Earth's environment is from outside it. The European Space Agency's ENVISAT satellite does just that, monitoring the planet using an array of 10 different instruments.

Put into orbit in early 2002, ENVISAT looks down upon the Earth from a distance of 790km (491 miles). It takes a 101-minute journey around the globe at an inclination of 90° to the Equator, and encompassing both poles. This is the optimum path for 'planet watching', giving the satellite the best viewpoint of both the globe and its environment.

Packed with technology

ENVISAT is the largest Earth-observation satellite ever built, and it is unlikely anything comparable of this size will ever be launched again. Its impressive size partly comes from the number of instruments it carries. Because its role is such a multifaceted one, involving looking at land, water, ice and atmosphere, it is equipped with 10 different monitoring tools. These include a radar that can detect variances in height down to a sub-millimetre, devices for measuring the temperature of the sea's surface as well as the amount of ice on it, a radiometer for measuring atmospheric water vapour, and, perhaps most significant of all in these days of environmental concern, an ozone monitor. It's also capable of capturing some pretty stunning photographs.

One of its more recent – and more amazing – uses was to monitor a huge crack that appeared in the Earth's surface in Ethiopia over three weeks in 2005. ENVISAT was able to measure the fissure, which was 8m (26ft) wide, and determine that it stretched for over 60km (37.3 miles), something it would have taken far longer to realize without the use of the environmental satellite.

SPECIFICATIONS

Country: Various (European Space Agency)

Year launched: 2002

Dimensions: 10m (33ft) long

Weight: 8211kg (8.2 tons)

Distance from Earth: 790km (491 miles)

Cost: Euros 2.3 billion

THE LARGEST REUSEABLE SPACECRAFT

SPACE SHUTTLE

NASA's Space Shuttle is by far the most famous (real) spacecraft of all time, a technical tour de force that goes into space like a conventional rocket, but lands like an aircraft. However, despite its practicality, the shuttle programme hasn't been without its problems.

As space mega machines go, the American Space Shuttle takes some beating. It was the first orbital vehicle to be reusable, and the only winged vehicle capable of going into space and returning again. It can carry up to eight astronauts, take extremely large payloads in its cargo bay and also recover items from space. Nothing else comes close to the sheer versatility of the Space Shuttle.

It was conceived during the 1970s, and there have been six shuttles in total. The first (named *Enterprise* after a campaign by *Star Trek* fans) was simply a test vehicle and never went into space. The other five (*Challenger, Columbia, Discovery, Atlantis* and *Endeavour*) have all been launched beyond Earth's atmosphere. The first take-off was on 12 April 1981, by *Columbia,* an event witnessed on TV by millions.

To obtain orbit, the Space Shuttle launches on top of an external fuel tank with booster rockets on either side. Once the boosters have fallen away, the fuel tank supplies the Space Shuttle's own engines until it, too, is detached. That leaves the shuttle alone once it reaches space. Upon re-entry into Earth's atmosphere, the craft just glides back to base, using no power whatsoever.

The shuttle has revolutionized space travel, but it has also highlighted just how dangerous it still is too. Two vehicles, *Columbia* and *Challenger,* have been destroyed in service, resulting in the loss of all crew.

SPECIFICATIONS

Country: USA
Year launched: 1981
Dimensions: 37m (122ft) long; 24m (78ft) wide
Weight (empty): 68,586kg (151,205lb)
Payload: 25,061kg (55,250lb)
Lift-off thrust: 3.076 million kgf
Cost: $174 billion (projected, by 2010)

LEFT AND ABOVE: As familiar and famous as the space shuttle is now, its re-usable nature – taking off the same way an ordinary spacecraft does, but then landing like a conventional aircraft (albeit a non-powered glider) – was radical when it was introduced.

THE LARGEST TRACKED VEHICLE

SPACE SHUTTLE CRAWLER

The Space Shuttle is extraordinary in its own right. However, mention must be made of the way it gets to the launch site. It travels there on the Crawler-Transporter, the largest non-engineering tracked vehicle around.

SPECIFICATIONS

Country: USA
Year built: 1967
Dimensions: 40m (131ft) long; 35m (114ft) wide
Weight: 2,700,000kg (2,976 tons)
Power: 2050kW (2750bhp)
Maximum speed: 3km/h (2mph)
Cost: $14 million

LEFT: Fast as the shuttle may be, the first part of any space shuttle trip requires one of these with a top speed of 1.6km/h (1mph).

Only the German Bagger 288 excavator has bigger tracks than the two Crawler-Transporters (nicknamed Hans and Fritz) used to carry the Space Shuttle (and its ancestor rockets) from its Vehicle Assembly Building at the Kennedy Space Center in Florida out to the launch pad. The distance is 5.6km (3.5 miles) but with a top speed of 1.6km/h (1mph) when laden – and only 3km/h (2mph) when returning unburdened – a crawler is hardly quick. Typically, a Space Shuttle will take between three and five hours to reach the pad. Any faster, and the craft would be in danger of toppling over, although the crawlers have a tilting platform to help prevent this. Because such vast vehicles can't be easily turned around, they have a cab on each end.

Slow 'n' thirsty

Despite the snail-like speed, the crawlers are immensely powerful. Two 2050kW (2750hp) engines drive the four generators and 16 traction motors that power the eight tracked sections (each pair the size of a Greyhound bus), two of which are in each corner of the crawler. However, it's a thirsty machine, with the average fuel consumption being 350 litre/km (150 US gallons per mile). To accommodate this, the tank on a crawler holds 19,000 litres (5000 US gallons) of fuel.

The Crawler-Transporters have been in operation since the Saturn V days, and will outlast the Space Shuttle and be used for the next generation of NASA spacecraft.

THE LARGEST COMMERCIAL SPACECRAFT

SPACESHIPONE

Prior to the twenty-first century, space was the preserve of only the richest nations that could afford the immense costs associated with travel into space. But by 2004 this was no longer the case, when SpaceShipOne (SS1) became the first privately funded spacecraft.

On 4 October 2004 (coincidentally the forty-seventh anniversary of the Sputnik launch), the space plane SS1 scooped the coveted Ansari X prize by becoming the first non-government funded reusable manned spacecraft to go into space twice within two weeks.

Undoubtedly, the award of $10 million was welcome, although SS1 had cost $25 million to develop (a miniscule amount compared to most programmes). But no doubt of far more significance to the Tier One team who built SS1 was that they had managed to go where nobody else in a private craft had gone before.

Piggyback into space

SS1 may have entered only the lower reaches of designated space, 100km (62 miles) up, but that was still enough to officially make it a spacecraft, albeit one actually registered as a glider, since most of its flight was not powered. The SS1 wasn't launched like the Space Shuttle, but instead 'piggybacked' up to 14km (8.7 miles) using a White Knight aircraft. The SS1 then detached and used its own rocket to reach space, achieving a speed of Mach 3 in the process. It came back down to Earth simply by gliding, albeit with its wings folded up, operating like a huge shuttlecock.

SS1 has retired now, and can be found on display at the Smithsonian Air and Space Museum in Washington DC. However, its successor (which flies in the same manner) is currently in development, with finance by Sir Richard's Branson's Virgin Group. Its aim is to start space flights carrying passengers from 2008.

SPECIFICATIONS

Country: USA
Year built: 2003
Dimensions: 5m (16ft 6in) long; 5m (16ft 6 in) wide
Weight: (Loaded) 3600kg (7937lb)
Top speed: Mach 3.09 (3518km/h/2186mph)
Rocket burn time: 87 seconds
Cost: $25 million

ABOVE AND BELOW: SpaceShipOne started its journey into space slung underneath a White Night aircraft, and used its own rocket only once it has detached at a height of 14km (8.7 miles).

LEFT AND BELOW: In orbit around the red planet, the MRO's current mission is to gather information on Mars, but it will eventually change role to become a control and communications point for future spacecraft from Earth.

THE LARGEST MARS PROBE

MARS RECONNAISSANCE ORBITER

The Mars Reconnaissance Orbiter (MRO) is the largest and latest of probes to be sent out to orbit the fourth planet from the Sun. Its aim is to collect data and smooth the way for any future missions to the Red Planet.

When the Mars Reconnaissance Orbiter achieved orbit around Mars in March 2006, after eight months of travel, it brought the number of spacecraft studying Mars to six, the largest for any planet ever before. However, the MRO is so advanced it could almost render the other probes redundant. In fact, its systems will be able to pass more data back to Earth than all the other Mars missions combined.

Martian map-making

Operations begun at the end of 2006, and one of the MRO's primary objectives is to map the Martian landscape in unprecedented detail using a high-definition camera, to aid scientists in finding suitable landing sites for future land vehicles. In addition, it will study the climate, weather, atmosphere and geology of the planet, using the array of eight scientific and engineering instruments on board. It is envisaged that this should take two years.

However, once these operations are over, the MRO will switch roles to become a communication and navigation hub for other craft visiting Mars. Its most prominent piece of equipment is the 3m (10ft) antenna mounted above its large solar panels. This is the most sophisticated telecommunications device ever sent into deep space, and should ensure that future Mars explorers are able to send and transmit messages to and from Earth easily and quickly.

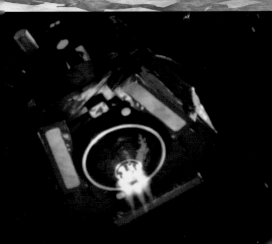

SPECIFICATIONS

Country: USA
Year launched: 2005
Dimensions: 7m (22ft) long; 13m (44ft) wide
Weight: 2180kg (4806lb)
Distance above Mars: Approximately 255–320km (160–200 miles)
Cost: $720 million

THE LARGEST GAS TURBINE JET

GENERAL ELECTRIC GE90-115B GAS TURBINE JET ENGINE

A jet engine as a work of art? Yes, if it's General Electric's GE90. In 2004, a fan blade from one was acquired by New York's Museum of Modern Art to put on display because it was regarded as such a beautiful piece of design work. The rest of the engine is pretty special, too, since it is the largest and most powerful gas turbine in existence.

ABOVE: Comparison with a man illustrates just how big and complicated the GE90-115B jet is. Just one of the black-finished, curved blades of the front fan was deemed an art form by NYC's Museum of Modern Art.

They may never have visited NYC's Museum of Modern Art, but many people will already be familiar with the GE90-115B turbine, even if they don't realize it. For the GE90 is the main engine choice for the Boeing 777 civil airliner, in service all over the world.

Guinness record holder

Introduced in 1995, and available only on 777s, the latest 115-B variant of the GE90 has its own entry in the *Guinness Book of Records* because it is so large and powerful, with a front fan diameter of 325cm (128in). The curved design is unique, and the black blades – one of its most distinctive features – comes from its composite material. The carbon-fibre polymeric construction is far lighter than the traditional titanium used on jet fans, and is able to help deliver a tremendous amount of thrust. For comparison purposes, one jet engine of a Boeing 747 can put out 289kN (65,000lbf) of thrust. The GE90 115-B has managed 569kN (127,900lbf).

Physically, the whole engine is so huge that it's bigger than the fuselage on a Boeing 737 (3.4m/11ft). And if a replacement engine has to be flown anywhere, it requires an ultra-large plane, like an Antonov An-124, to carry it.

SPECIFICATIONS

Country:	USA
Year built:	1995 onwards
Dimensions:	7.3m (24ft) long; 3.43m (11ft) diameter
Weight:	8282.6kg (9 tons)
Max thrust:	569kN (127,900lbf)
Number of fan blades:	22
Cost:	N/A

THE LARGEST AND MOST POWERFUL DIESEL ENGINE

WARTSILA -SULZER RTA96-C DIESEL ENGINES

Forget about using this diesel engine in a car, truck or train. The world's largest and most powerful diesel engine is about the size of a house and weighs over 2,300,000kg (2535 tons), and is used primarily for powering the biggest container ships.

ABOVE: An RTA96-C during construction, the gigantic crankshaft moves the pistons up and down.

Not many diesel engines have flights of steps installed so that mechanics and engineers can reach their parts. But at almost 26m (85ft) in length and 13m (43ft) tall, not many diesel engines are like Wartsila-Sulzer's RTA96-C series. Available in 6- through to 14-cylinder versions, these turbocharged, very tough mechanical monsters are the biggest reciprocating engines in the world, with the ultimate 14-cylinder version putting out a whopping 81,221.6kW (108,920hp). As container ships grow ever greater in size, the engine powering them also has to grow to meet these increasing requirements, especially as many companies prefer the simplicity of a single engine/single propeller set-up within their vessels.

The power of 3747 Rolls-Royces!

To compare the 14-cylinder model to an 'ordinary' engine is like contrasting a skyscraper with a shed. The current Rolls-Royce Phantom motorcar has what is regarded as a quite substantial powerplant of 6.8 litres (415cu in). The capacity of the RTA96-C is 25,480 litres (1,556,002cu in), which represents 3747 Phantoms all working together! All the RTA96-C types are built to run on cheap, low-grade fuel but, despite this, they're still far from cheap to run, with fuel consumption at around 7,546 litres (1660 gallons) of diesel fuel per hour on the 14-cylinder example. And that's at its most efficient setting!

THE LARGEST TELEVISION

SONY POWER TRON TV

Televisions are just getting bigger and bigger. Recent innovations in liquid crystal display (LCD) technology have meant larger and flatter screens in our homes than ever before. But the home system of the future will still have some way to go to beat the world's most substantial TV screen, set up near Tokyo, Japan.

ABOVE: With a screen this big, it's difficult not to get a good view. However, the equivalent remote control must be difficult to handle.

There are two main players in the contest to be called the world's largest TV. One is the Diamond Vision display, built by Mitsubishi at the Hong Kong Jockey Club, which is as long as a Jumbo Jet – widescreen TV indeed. It measures 70.4m (231ft) across, and is used to show three different views of a race at once. However, in height, it is only 8m (26ft) tall, which means it can't quite compare to the Sony Power Tron installation in Japan – that was as tall as an eight-storey building.

International showcase

Although giant Power Tron screens have seen much use at major events – one at which they usually feature is New Year in Times Square, New York City – none have surpassed the one that was unveiled in March 1985 in Tsukuba near Tokyo in Japan. Erected as part of the International Exposition held there, it measured 24.3m (80ft) high by 46m (150ft) across and showed specially made videos and artworks.

Because it stood outside and needed to be seen against daylight, Sony used large fluorescent tubes – like office lights – to boost the picture. However, its pixel resolution – of 378 vertical by 400 horizontal – left a little to be desired in picture clarity. By contrast, the newer, more advanced Mitsubishi Diamond Vision LCD rival has a pixel count of 400 x 3520.

SPECIFICATIONS	
Country: Japan	
Year built: 1985	
Dimensions: 24m (80ft) tall; 46m (150ft) across	
Cost: N/A	

THE LARGEST LIFT BRIDGE

AERIAL BRIDGE, DULUTH

Originally built as a transporter bridge in 1905, the Aerial Bridge in Duluth, Minnesota, USA, was converted into a vertical lift bridge 25 years after traffic outgrew its capabilities. Today, it is still the world's largest of the type, as well as the fastest.

BELOW: The Duluth Aerial Bridge, with its lower deck lifted to allow a passenger ship to travel underneath.

In 1870, a small canal was created near the port city of Duluth. One of the side effects of this was the creation of an inhabited island, whose residents had no way of crossing the water, with both ferries and a swinging footbridge affected by the weather.

From transporter to lift

The solution was to build a transporter bridge. This was fine for a few years until it simply became unable to cope with the rapid growth around Duluth. A solution had to be found but one that was able to still allow tall ships to use the canal.

Thus, in 1930, the transporter structure was reworked into a lifting bridge, with a deck that could be moved up and down as required. A new deck was fitted, with counterweights installed into the original towers to balance it. This is the set-up that still remains in operation, lifting between 25 to 30 times a day during busy periods. When the main deck is lowered, it sits a mere 4.6m (15ft) above the water. After 55 seconds (the time it takes to raise fully), the deck can be at 42m (138ft) – although without any cars or people on it, obviously.

The bridge has become Duluth's main tourist attraction and it was listed as a national historic monument in 1973.

SPECIFICATIONS

Country: USA
Year built: 1905, converted 1930
Dimensions: 118m (386ft) long; 69m (227ft) tall
Weight: 816,466kg (900 tons)
Lifting speed: 37.5m (123ft) per minute
Cost: $100,000 (original transporter bridge)

LONDON EYE

The British Airways London Eye, also known as the Millennium Wheel, is one of the UK capital's newest landmarks, standing on the bank of the River Thames close to the Houses of Parliament. As the largest Ferris wheel ever built, it gives tourists amazing views over the city and its many other familiar sights.

The end of the twentieth century saw many new projects instigated to mark the passing of the millennium. Probably the most high profile and successful in the United Kingdom was the London Eye observation wheel. It took seven years to come to fruition, being officially opened by the British prime minister on New Year's Eve, 1999. With a height of 135m (443ft), it can be seen from all over the capital, and can let those riding in its cars see all over the capital, too.

Keep on going

When loading passengers – 800 can ride at any one time – the wheel never stops revolving. But as it travels at only 0.9km/h (0.6mph), it's easy enough for passengers to walk on and off at the wide platforms at the bottom of the structure. A complete revolution takes around 30 minutes to complete. However, because the Eye keeps turning, its cars notch up a huge 3,392,000km (2,107,749 miles) over the course of an average year. That's the equivalent of going to the moon and back 4.4 times! The pods turn within circular mounting rings fixed to the outside of the main frame, ensuring a 360° view.

Like that other great European 'temporary' structure, Paris' Eiffel Tower, the Millennium Wheel was never intended to be permanent. It had planning permission for only five years originally, but such was its popularity – it carries 3.5 million people a year – that it has now become permanent.

LEFT: The tall London Eye can be glimpsed from all over the city, especially when illuminated at night. It's a mesmerizing sight.

SPECIFICATIONS

Country: UK

Year: 1998–1999

Dimensions: 135m (443ft) tall, wheel circumference 424m (1392ft)

Number of cars: 32

Passenger capacity: 800

Speed: 0.9km/h (0.6mph)

Weight: 2,100,000kg (2314 tons)

Cost: £75 million

ABOVE AND LEFT: Ride the London Eye on a clear day, and the view from the top can stretch for 40km (25 miles).

INDEX